Spain Live

Isabel Alonso de Sudea
Kit Davies

OXFORD
UNIVERSITY PRESS

OXFORD
UNIVERSITY PRESS

Great Clarendon Street, Oxford OX2 6DP

Oxford University Press is a department of the University of Oxford. It furthers the University's objective of excellence in research, scholarship, and education by publishing worldwide in

Oxford New York

Auckland Cape Town Dar es Salaam Hong Kong Karachi Kuala Lumpur Madrid Melbourne Mexico City Nairobi New Delhi Shanghai Taipei Toronto

With offices in

Argentina Austria Brazil Chile Czech Republic France Greece Guatemala Hungary Italy Japan Poland Portugal Singapore South Korea Switzerland Thailand Turkey Ukraine Vietnam

Oxford is a registered trade mark of Oxford University Press in the UK and in certain other countries

Based on an original idea by Sue Finnie and Danièle Bourdais

The moral rights of the authors have been asserted

Database right Oxford University Press (maker)

First published 2004

British Library Cataloguing in Publication Data

Data available

ISBN-13: 978-0-19-912495-4
ISBN-10: 0-19-912495-7

10 9 8 7 6 5 4 3 2

Printed in Italy by Rotolito Lombarda

Acknowledgements

The publishers would like to thank the following for their permission to reproduce photographs:

Cover: Comstock, Dick Capel-Davies, El Pais website, Iconotec, Imagesource, Mixa Image Library

Title page: Comstock.

1dpi Ltd: **pp32** (bottom), **50** (top); Alamy/David Sanger Photography: **pp8** (top), **30** (top); Alamy/Eric James: **p47** (right); Alamy/Image state: **p26** (bottom left); Alamy/John Arnold Images: **pp46** (left), **48** (right), **55**; Alamy/John Harding Images: **p28** (left middle bottom); Alamy/Art Kowalsky: **p51** (middle); Alamy/Lightroom Photos: **p44** (bottom); Alamy/Sergio Pitamitz: **p49**; Alamy/Robert Harding Picture Library Ltd: **pp14** (bottom), **33** (bottom right); Alamy/Ray Roberts: **pp28** (middle right), **48** (left), **66** (bottom); Alamy/Mick Rock: **p40** (top); Alamy/Alex Segre: **p15**; Alamy/World Religions Photo Library: **p29** (left); Alamy/David Wooton: **p28** (bottom right); Alamy/David Young-Wolff: **p6** (bottom right); Archivo Oronoz: **pp14** (top left), **33** (middle right), **39** (top); Associated Press **pp52** (top), **69**; Bridgeman Art Library: **pp57** (bottom), **58** (middle), **66** (right); Corbis Sygma/Annebicque Bernard: **p68**; Corbis Sygma/Brisson Daniel **p54** (bottom); Corbis Sygma/Pavlovsky Jacques: **p75** (top); Corbis Sygma/J B Russel: **p70**; Corbis UK Ltd/Fernando Alda: **p6** (middle left); Corbis UK Ltd/Paul Almasy: **pp6** (middle), **19**, **47** (top); Corbis UK Ltd/Archivo Iconografico, S.A: **pp6** (top right), **36** (bottom), **57** (top); Corbis UK Ltd/Manuel Bellver: **p14** (middle left); Corbis UK/Bettmann: **pp58** (top), **66** (left); Corbis UK Ltd/Jonathan Blair: **p8** (centre); Corbis UK Ltd/Richard Bickel: **p8** (bottom); Corbis UK Ltd/Michael Busselle: **p43** (middle); Corbis UK Ltd/Michelle Chaplow: **pp45** (right), **62**; Corbis/Stephanie Colasanti: **p47** (left); Corbis UK Ltd/Dusko Despotovic: **p65** (bottom); Corbis/Eye Ubiquitous/Christopher J Hall: **p50** (middle); Corbis UK Ltd/ Eye Ubiquitous/David Forman: **p35** (bottom); Corbis UK Ltd/Eye Ubiquitous/Paul Seheult: **p46** (bottom); Corbis UK Ltd/Owen Franken: **pp23** (left), **25** (right), **40** (bottom right), **52** (bottom); Corbis UK Ltd/Eric & David Hosking: **p51** (bottom); Corbis UK Ltd/Frank Lane Picture Agency/Fritz Polking: **p43** (bottom); Corbis UK Ltd/Jose Fuste Raga: **pp28** (top left), **37**; Corbis UK Ltd/Isosport: **p20**; Corbis UK Ltd/John Henley Photography: **p17**; Corbis UK Ltd/Kelly-Mooney Photography: **p16**; Corbis UK Ltd/Richard Klune: **p35** (top); Corbis UK Ltd/Abilio Lope: **p50** (bottom); Corbis UK Ltd/Rob Matheson: **p21** (bottom); Corbis UK Ltd/Gideon Mendel: **pp10**, **74** (top); Corbis UK Ltd/Gianni Dagli Orti: **p56** (top); Corbis UK Ltd/Galen Rowell: **p14** (top right); Corbis UK Ltd/James Sparshatt: **p46** (middle right); Corbis UK Ltd/Patrick Ward: **p31** (right); Corbis UK Ltd: **pp5** (left & right), **18**, **36** (top); Corbis UK Ltd/Adam Woolfitt: **p33** (bottom left); Getty Images: **pp56** (bottom), **58** (bottom); Hemera Technologies: **pp6** (bottom left), **30** (top right), **64** (bottom left); Iconotec: **pp6** (middle right), **30** (bottom), **34**, **73** (top); Magnum Photos/Stuart Franklin: **p43** (top); Magnum Photos/David Alan Harvey: **p71**; Milepost: **p54** (top); Mixa Image Library: **pp14** (middle right), **44** (top), **72** (top left); Photostore/M.Graff: **p32** (top); Rex Features Ltd/Action Press: **pp41**, **60** (bottom); Rex Features Ltd/Miguel Benitez: **pp23** (right), **59**; Rex Features Ltd/Nils Jorgensen: **p22** (top); Rex Features Ltd/Crollalanza: **p67**; Rex Features Ltd/Saukkomaa: **p45** (bottom left); R.E.F.E. 1979 Rex Features Ltd/Sipa Press: **pp45** (top), **60** (top); Rex Features Ltd/Richard Sowersby: **p40** (bottom left); Rex Features Ltd/Ray Tang: **p73** (middle left); Rex Features Ltd/Crispin Thruston: **p22** (centre); Rex Features Ltd/R. Young: **p22** (bottom); Science Photo Library/Simon Fraser: **p74** (middle); Science Photo Library/Chris Sattleberger: **p75** (bottom); David Simson: **pp27** (bottom left & right), **28** (left middle top) **28** (top right), **29** (right); Martin Sookias: **p73** (middle right); Spanish Tourism Board: **pp14** (top & centre middle), **27** (top left & right), **28** (bottom left), **33** (top left), **51** (top); Travel Ink/Ronald Badkin: **p33** (top right).

All other photographs are by Isabel Alonso de Sudea.

Illustrations are by:
James Arnold (cartoons) and Stefan Chabluk (maps).

Every effort has been made to contact copyright holders of material reproduced in this book. Any omissions will be rectified in subsequent printings if notice is given to the publisher.

Introduction

Spain Live is a culture book for school-age students of Spanish. It comprises 18 chapters covering a range of relevant and interesting topics.

Spain Live will help meet the aims of the QCA Scheme of Work and the Cultural knowledge and Contact strand of the Modern Languages Framework. It can be used alongside any course book, and the differentiated material makes it ideal for students working at different levels.

Contents

1 ¡Viva España! ... 4
2 Family life ... 8
3 House and home ... 12
4 School life ... 16
5 Leisure ... 20
6 Food and drink ... 24
7 Festivals and traditions ... 28
8 Geography ... 32
9 The people of Spain ... 36
10 In the country ... 40
11 In town ... 44
12 Madrid ... 48
13 Travel and transport ... 52
14 History ... 56
15 How Spain is governed today ... 60
16 The media and the arts ... 64
17 Working in Spain ... 68
18 Industry and commerce ... 72
Map of Spain ... 76
Map of the Spanish-speaking world ... 77
Useful Spanish websites ... 78
Index ... 79

1 ¡Viva España!

What does the image of Spain mean for you? Sun, sand, sea, sangria and siesta, or fiestas, flamenco and football?

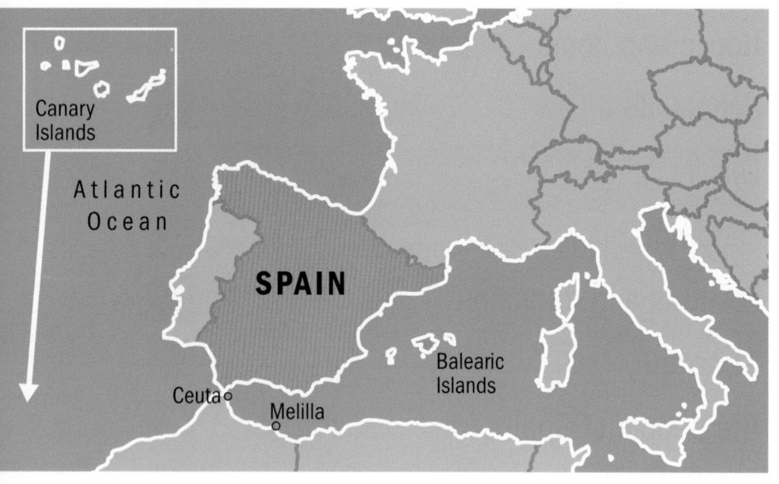

When Spanish people talk of Spain they don't just mean the country which forms 80% of the Iberian Peninsula (Portugal accounts for the remaining 20%). Spain also includes the four Balearic Islands of Mallorca, Menorca, Ibiza and Formentera, the seven Canary Islands, Ceuta, Melilla, and several very small islands off the coast of Morocco. Spaniards tend not to speak of *España* but rather *Las Españas* or *El Reino de España* (the Kingdom of Spain). Spain is sometimes called 'the old bull's hide'.

Spain is the second largest country in size in Europe, after France, and has the fifth largest population. To the north the Pyrenees form a natural barrier between Spain and the countries of France and Andorra. Spain has more than 2200 km of mainland coastline – the Cantabrian Sea and the Bay of Biscay to the north, the Atlantic Ocean to the east and the Mediterranean to the south and west. Throughout its history, Spain has been an important cultural bridge between Europe and Africa. They are just 16 km apart!

How does it compare?

Surface area

Country	Area
Spain	504 750 km^2
France	550 000 km^2
Germany	504 750 km^2
UK	244 000 km^2

With five mountain ranges and a high plateau *(meseta)*, Spain is the highest country in Europe after Switzerland, at an average of 650 metres above sea level. Spain's landscapes vary from rich green valleys in the north topped by the oldest mountains in Europe (the *Picos de Europa* and also the Pyrenees), to wide high plains in the centre and bare rugged mountains in the south. The longest river is the Ebro, which takes its name from the earliest settlers, the Ibers.

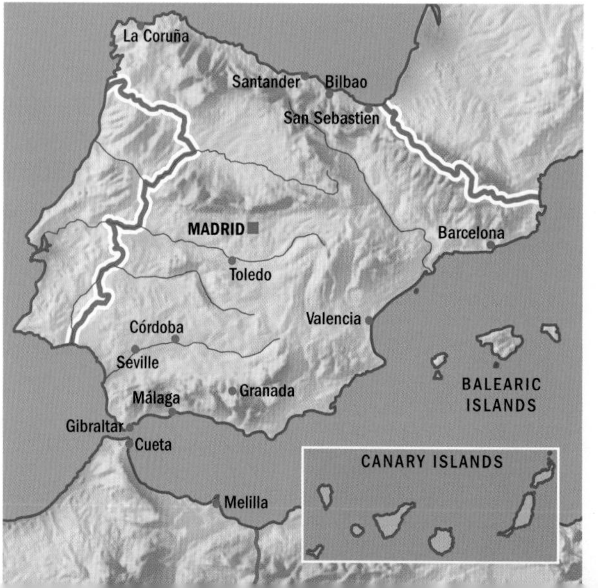

One key thing to remember throughout this book is how much and how quickly Spain has changed in the last thirty years or so, at the same time as maintaining and honouring its old traditions and customs.

Population

Spain: 40 million
UK: 60 million
France: 62 million
Germany: 82 million

Capital

Madrid: 5.42 million
London: 12 million
Paris: 10.9 million
Berlin: 3.45 million

Other main cities

Barcelona: 4.80 million
Valencia: 2.22 million
Seville: 1.73 million

Greater Manchester: 2.5 million
Birmingham: 1 million

A world language

Spanish is the official language of twenty-three countries and is spoken worldwide as a first language by some 350 million people. It is the world's most important commercial language after English and the third most widely spoken after Chinese and English (see the map on page 77).

A wonderful host

Spain has a huge tourist population – the highest in Europe. More than 50 million people visit Spain each year, of whom 14 million are from the UK. When you consider that the population of Spain is only 40 million, it means more people visit the country than live there permanently.

Many different nationalities live in Spain, mostly from Morocco and Latin America, and there is a growing number of British residents (about two million). Most live on the coast – *la costa* (see Chapter 9).

Remember, Spain is one hour ahead of the UK and uses the metric system.

Spain used to be governed with a firm hand from Madrid, the capital, which lies at the centre of the country, but all that has changed. Today, Spain is divided into seventeen self-governing, administrative areas called *Comunidades Autónomas (CCAA)*, each with its own capital city and flag (see Chapter 15).

Read the information on pages 4 and 5 and complete the quiz.

1 **a** Write down five things you knew about Spain before you started to read this chapter. Now write down five things you have learnt and compare your notes with a partner.

b Why do you think Spain is called 'the old bull's hide'?

c How many people in the world speak Spanish as a first language?

2 Use your dictionary and write down, in Spanish, the names of the countries that border Spain and the seas that surround it. Can you do the same for the UK?

3 Write a short paragraph (about 50 words) on the following:

a In what way is Spain different from the UK?

b What do you like about Spain and why?

Saint James is the patron saint of Spain.

Land of surprises

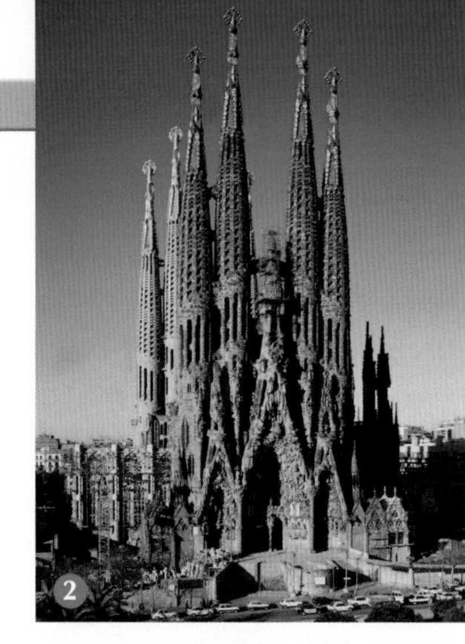

Perhaps the biggest surprise for someone coming to Spain for the first time is its regional diversity of language, cultural heritage, artistic traditions, landscapes and politics. The monuments in Spain reflect some of its history: from the Romans and Moors, the discovery of the Americas by Christopher Columbus (Cristóbal Colón) and the sixteenth century, when Spain ruled most of what we call Europe today, to the austere, suppressed thirty years of the dictator Franco's regime and the modern icons of the twenty-first century.

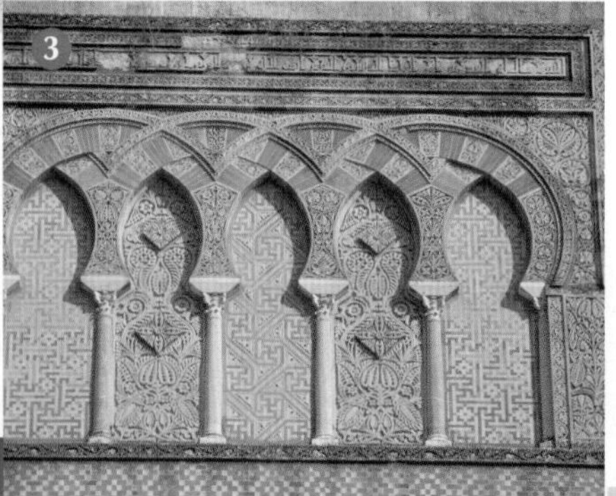

1 Roman theatre, Merida
2 Sagrada Familia, Barcelona
3 Mosque, Cordoba
4 Salamanca
5 Calatrava's bridge, Seville
6 Guggenheim museum, Bilbao

The peseta used to be the currency of Spain until it was replaced by the euro in January 2000.

Flags

The Spanish national flag has three horizontal bands (red, yellow (double width), and red) and the royal coat of arms, which is framed by the Pillars of Hercules guarding the entrance to the Mediterranean.

Each autonomous region has its own flag, which can be seen on most public buildings alongside the national flag (see page 61).

Parliamentary monarchy

Spain has a royal family with King Juan Carlos I as the Head of State. The Spanish monarchy costs taxpayers about half as much as Britain's, and less than any in Europe. Members of the Royal Family pay taxes.

The languages of Spain

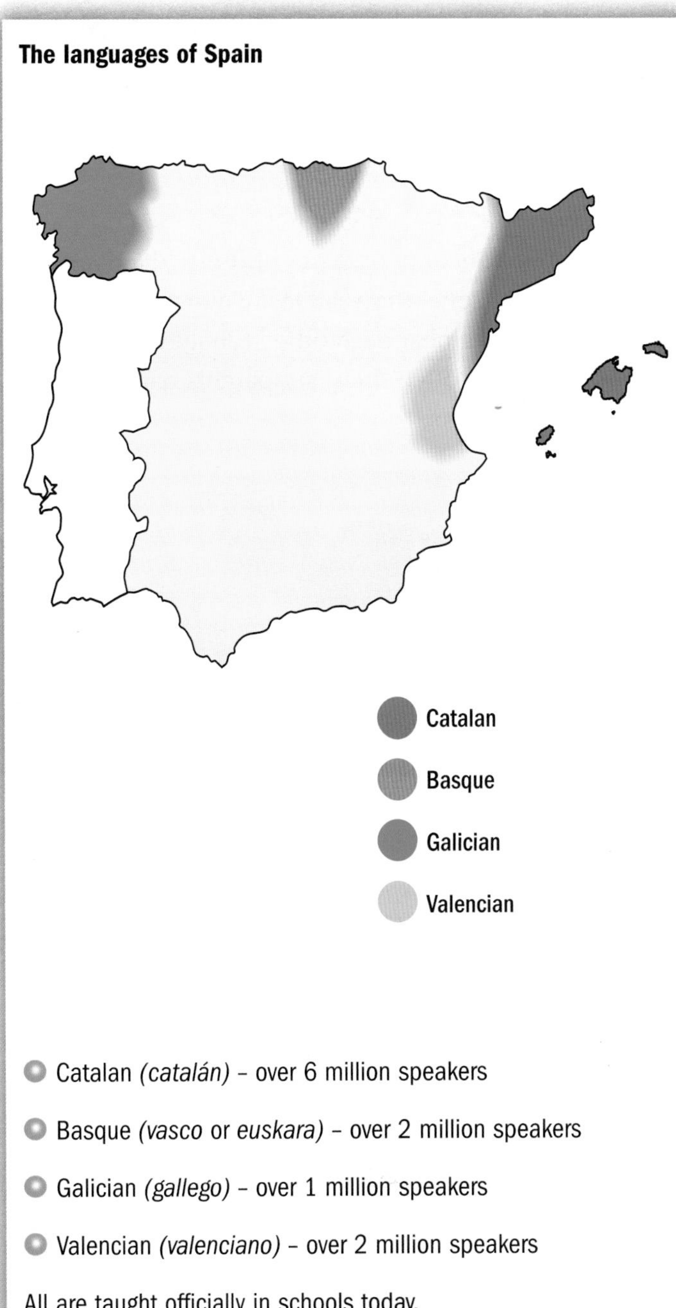

- Catalan *(catalán)* – over 6 million speakers
- Basque *(vasco* or *euskara)* – over 2 million speakers
- Galician *(gallego)* – over 1 million speakers
- Valencian *(valenciano)* – over 2 million speakers

All are taught officially in schools today.

Life on display

In Spain you live life to the full. Spaniards have an infectious enthusiasm for life so there is always something going on out in the streets *(en la calle)*, even in winter. Today, Spain is as well known for its lively arts scene as it is for its fiestas. Spaniards are justifiably proud of their artistic culture, and Picasso, Miró and Dalí are as widely promoted as film stars and pop stars.

Spain's national holiday

An important date for the Spanish-speaking world is 12 October – *el Día de la Raza* or *el Día de la Hispanidad* – when people celebrate the discovery of the Americas by Christopher Columbus in 1492.

In 1992, 500 years later, Spain celebrated by hosting the Olympic games in Barcelona, the World Expo in Seville, and Madrid was European Capital of Culture. It also hosted the Sepharad, a cultural festival to welcome back the Jewish race 500 years after their expulsion from Spain.

Although the **official language** of Spain is Spanish (referred to as either *castellano* – Castilian, or *español* – Spanish), there are several other languages spoken in the regional autonomies. During Franco's rule these languages were suppressed as a threat to moral stability and law and order, but today this linguistic diversity is encouraged.

Read the information on pages 6 and 7 and complete the quiz.

1. a What does the emblem on the Spanish flag represent?
   b Who is the Head of State in Spain?
   c Why is 12 October an important date in Spain?
2. Who were Picasso, Miró and Dalí? Research some facts on the Internet or in the library.
3. Work with a partner and write a paragraph about the following:
   a What periods mark Spain's history? Can you name similar periods for the UK? What monuments are left from these times?
   b In your opinion, how important is it to keep regional languages and customs alive? Does the UK have regional divisions?

2 Family life

Traditionally, Spaniards have two surnames, using both the father's first family name and the mother's second family name. When a woman marries she drops the mother's family name and adds her husband's father's family name to her own father's name. So, when Susana López Navarro marries Tomás Alonso Guerra, she becomes Susana López de Alonso.

Greetings

Men usually shake hands when they meet, and take their leave formally.

Men and women who know each other usually kiss or embrace.

Children always kiss adults hello and goodbye.

It is no exaggeration to say that the family comes first in Spain. Spain has one of the highest numbers of people per household in Europe. It is not unusual to find several generations all living and working together under one roof, or living near each other. Families naturally show respect for their elders and often the grandparents have a hand in bringing up the younger children.

Family occasions

As in most countries, a wedding *(una boda)* brings families together. A wedding ring is worn on the fourth finger of the right hand in Spain. It is traditional to name children after the father, mother or grandparents and this often involves a saint's name as well. Spaniards celebrate their birthday *(el cumpleaños)* and their saint's day *(el santo)*.

Children are the centre of attention in a Spanish family so christenings *(un bautizo)* and first communions *(la primera comunión)* mean a family gathering usually accompanied by a large meal. Spaniards tend to spend a lot of money on these celebrations.

Pets

Spanish people are not very sentimental about pets *(el animal de compañía* or *la mascota)*. Traditionally, animals worked the land and provided food. On many balconies you may hear caged songbirds such as canaries. Today, dogs are becoming a status symbol but they have to be registered and wear a tattooed registration number or microchip. They have to have a health card, be kept on a lead in public places and are forbidden in places where food is served or sold. It is also illegal not to clean up after your dog and you can be fined on the spot!

Nicknames

Spanish people often use nicknames, which are shortened versions of the proper names. However, these tend to be restricted to informal situations.

Common boys' nicknames

Paco - Francisco
Pepe - José
Tito - Eduardo
Lucho - Luís

Common girls' nicknames

Chava chavelita - Isabel
Pili - Pilar
Merche - Mercedes
Conchi - Concepción
Pacha - Juana

People often add *-ito/-ita* to the end of names, especially when referring to small children, for example, Isabelita, Juanito.

They often use Don or Doña before the name of an older person, for example, Don Pedro, Doña Inés.

Daily routine

Naturally, routines differ slightly depending on whether you live in the country or city, and whether it is winter or summer. However, for most families the weekday begins at about 7am with a breakfast of coffee *(un café con leche)* and fresh bread *(pan fresco)* or cereals *(cereales)*. Sometimes people rub tomatoes and olive oil into the bread *(pan con tomate)* or, especially on Sundays, they might have *chocolate con churros* as a treat (see detail on page 24).

School *(el colegio)* starts at 9am and children often catch a school bus to get there. The younger ones may go to a crèche *(una guardería)* if their grandparents can't look after them.

Unless they work in a city (with air conditioning in the summer), most people in offices, shops and state schools break at 2pm and go home for lunch. After a family lunch, life comes to a halt for siesta time.

Things start to get going again at about 5pm. Young people often go to after-school clubs or to the local sports hall *(el polideportivo)*. Otherwise, they stay at home doing homework *(los deberes* or *las tareas)*, watch television *(ver la tele)* or play on the computer *(el ordenador)* or with video games *(los videojuegos)*.

Families eat dinner late – at about 8.30pm or even later at weekends. Often, they sit outside on the *terraza* or in the doorway of the street in villages and simply enjoy the cool of the evening while the children play around, or sit and chat. In cities and in the winter most families will watch television or listen to the radio.

Spaniards go to bed late by UK standards – at about midnight during the week and often much later at weekends.

Read the information on pages 8 and 9 and complete the quiz.

1 a What occasions bring families together in Spain? Write down the Spanish words for these occasions.
   b Explain to a friend how Spanish surnames work.
   c What sort of pets do Spanish people have? How does this compare with you, or with the UK in general?

2 Discuss or write a short paragraph about the following:
   a Compare the daily routine of a typical Spanish family with your own. Discuss the similarities and differences with a partner.
   b What do you think about the idea of having a siesta?

Average ages at which women and men leave home:

	Women	Men
Spain	26.6	28.4
Germany	21.6	24.8
France	22.2	24.1
UK	21.2	23.5

In a recent survey, 98% of people under 60 chose family over work, friends, leisure, religion or politics as being the single most important thing in their lives.

Young people tend to live at home longer (about 70% of 18–29 year olds according to a recent study), whether by tradition, desire or because house prices are too high. In addition, young people who have never been employed do not qualify for benefit.

The elderly *(la tercera edad)* are well looked after (they have the highest pensions in Europe after Sweden) and most towns have centres where people organise regular activities and outings for them. Increasingly, they are choosing to live in sheltered accommodation or a retirement home. The family nearly always lives close by and visits regularly.

Under Franco's rule divorce was not allowed, but in 1981 it was finally legalised. Even though Spain has a fairly liberal divorce law, it still has a low divorce rate. More often than not, couples separate but do not divorce, as it is hard to get payment of alimony.

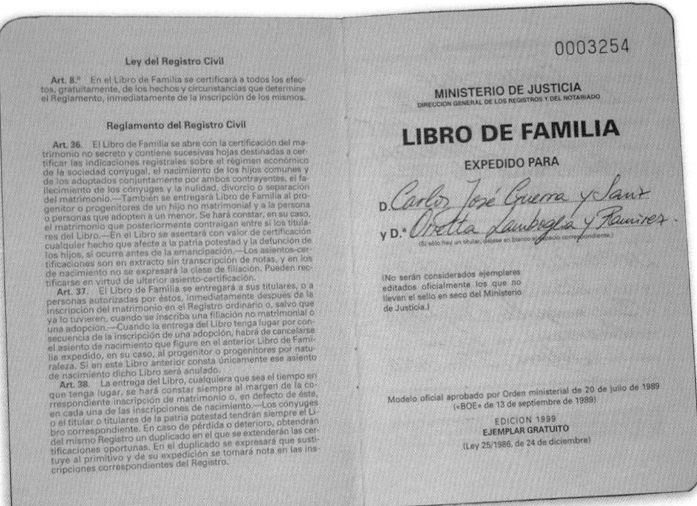

Ley del Registro Civil

Art. 8.º En el Libro de Familia se certificará a todos los efectos, gratuitamente, de los hechos y circunstancias que determine el Reglamento, inmediatamente de la inscripción de los mismos.

Reglamento del Registro Civil

Art. 36. El Libro de Familia se abre con la certificación del matrimonio no secreto y contiene sucesivas hojas destinadas a certificar las indicaciones registrales sobre el régimen económico de la sociedad conyugal, el nacimiento de los hijos comunes y de los adoptados conjuntamente por ambos contrayentes, el fallecimiento de los cónyuges y la nulidad, divorcio o separación del matrimonio.—También se entregará Libro de Familia al progenitor o progenitores de un hijo no matrimonial y a la persona o personas que adopten a un menor. Se hará constar, en su caso, el matrimonio que posteriormente contraigan entre sí los titulares del Libro.—En el Libro se asentará con valor de certificación cualquier hecho que afecte a la patria potestad y la defunción de los hijos, si ocurre antes de la emancipación.—Los asientos-certificaciones son en extracto sin transcripción de notas, y en los de nacimiento no se expresará la clase de filiación. Pueden rectificarse en virtud de ulterior asiento-certificación.

Art. 37. El Libro de Familia se entregará a sus titulares, o a personas autorizadas por éstos, inmediatamente después de la inscripción del matrimonio en el Registro ordinario o, salvo que ya lo tuvieren, cuando se inscriba una filiación no matrimonial o una adopción.—Cuando la entrega del Libro tenga lugar por consecuencia de la inscripción de una adopción, habrá de cancelarse el asiento de nacimiento que figure en el anterior Libro de Familia expedido, en su caso, al progenitor o progenitores por naturaleza. Si en este Libro anterior consta únicamente ese asiento de nacimiento dicho Libro será anulado.

Art. 38. La entrega del Libro, cualquiera que sea el tiempo en que tenga lugar, se hará constar siempre al margen de la correspondiente inscripción de matrimonio o, en defecto de éste, en cada una de las inscripciones de nacimiento.—Los cónyuges o el titular o titulares de la patria potestad tendrán siempre el Libro correspondiente. En caso de pérdida o deterioro, obtendrán del mismo Registro un duplicado en el que se extenderán las certificaciones oportunas. En el duplicado se expresará que sustituye al primitivo y de su expedición se tomará nota en las inscripciones correspondientes del Registro.

0003254

MINISTERIO DE JUSTICIA
DIRECCION GENERAL DE LOS REGISTROS Y DEL NOTARIADO

LIBRO DE FAMILIA

EXPEDIDO PARA

D. Carlos José Guerra y Sanz
y D.ª Orietta Lamboglia y Ramírez

(Si sólo hay un titular, déjese en blanco el espacio correspondiente.)

(No serán considerados ejemplares editados oficialmente los que no lleven el sello en seco del Ministerio de Justicia.)

Modelo oficial aprobado por Orden ministerial de 20 de julio de 1989 («BOE» de 13 de septiembre de 1989)

EDICION 1999
EJEMPLAR GRATUITO
(Ley 25/1986, de 24 de diciembre)

When couples marry they receive a family book *(un libro de familia)* – an official registration for the couple and their children. They need to present this when their children reach the age of fourteen in order to get them their identity cards *(Documento Nacional de Identidad* or *DNI)*. The family book is also used to get a social security card, to marry or divorce, and when someone dies. It is illegal to be without some form of identification.

From 1961 to 1973, many families were split up when well over a million Spaniards received assistance to go and work abroad in order to boost the economy. Many also migrated from the countryside to big cities. It was not unusual for a family to be living off the wages of one family member who was sending money home. Now, many of them have returned, bringing with them a European outlook on life and work. Spain still has a very unevenly distributed population, with overcrowding in the big cities and vast areas of the countryside deserted (see Chapter 10).

Spain is no longer officially a Catholic country and only 43% of the population regularly goes to church.

	Life expectancy *Male*	*Female*	Infant mortality (% of births)	Number of children per family
Spain	77	82	3.9	1.3
UK	75	80	5.5	1.6
France	75	80	4.6	1.9
Germany	74	80	4.5	1.35

Traditional large families are a thing of the past. Since 1977, when contraception was officially permitted in Spain, the birth rate has slowed dramatically. Today, the national average is 1.3 children per family. Spain has the lowest marriage rate in Europe and also the lowest birth rate. The population is growing older, with about 20% of the population over 65 years old. The under 14s only make up about 15% of the total population. Spain has one of the highest levels of life expectancy and one of the lowest rates of infant mortality in Europe.

The State looks after families well in Spain. Until very recently, most Spaniards enjoyed high social security benefits. Article 43 of the Spanish Constitution of 1978 says that all Spaniards have the right to health treatment. Most people belong to a scheme called INSALUD, the National Health System, and the provision is one of the best in Europe. Today, helicopters are used in emergencies, as well as ambulances, mainly because of the large distances between towns.

Alcoholism has never really been a major problem in Spain. People eat when they drink and don't just drink to get drunk. However, smoking, especially amongst younger women, and drugs have become a major problem in Spain. Recently, campaigns such as *Proyecto Hombre* have had some success, and drug dealers and users are dealt with harshly.

Interestingly, the crime rate in Spain is one of the lowest in Europe, though it has begun to rise in the last decade. Most Spanish people show respect for 'law and order', though not for what they consider to be 'unimportant' bylaws such as parking restrictions! In villages, most people don't even lock their doors.

Read the information on pages 10 and 11 and complete the quiz.

1 Why do young people tend to live at home longer in Spain than in the UK? Do you think that this is a good idea?
2 What is the main religion in Spain? What are the main religions in the UK?
3 When was divorce permitted in Spain? Why was it not allowed before?
4 What happened to families during the 1960s?
5 What is happening to the birth rate in Spain?
6 What health campaigns are there in Spain? How does this compare with the UK?

3 House and home

A modern apartment in town

A house in the country

The standard of living has risen greatly in Spain in the last thirty years or so and this is very much reflected in the home. Many Spaniards own their homes. Today, less than 12% live in rented accommodation, the lowest level in Europe.

Many people in urban areas live in apartment blocks *(edificios)*, both old and modern. Many also have a second home in the country that has often belonged to the family for generations.

Modern apartments *(los pisos)* usually have a garage *(un garaje)* and a store room *(un trastero)* in the basement *(el sotano)*. They also have a balcony *(un balcón)*, modern kitchen *(una cocina moderna)* and a washing area *(un lavadero)*, which overlooks the open space of the interior *(el patio de la luz* – see right). Today, they have central heating *(calefacción central)* and air conditioning *(aire acondicionado)*, or often an open fire *(una chimenea)*. On the outskirts of towns and cities, a lot of town houses *(chalets* or *casas adosadas)* are being built.

In times gone by, a large metal bowl *(el brasero)* was filled with red-hot coals and put under the table. The family would sit around the table with their legs and feet under a long tablecover, being warmed by the hot coals.

Similarities and differences

- Bathrooms generally only have showers and bidets.
- Fitted carpets are not very common as houses and apartments are tiled throughout.
- Vacuum cleaners are not really necessary – tiled floors are easily mopped and cleaned daily.
- Just like in the UK, kitchens are equipped with fridges, washing machines, dishwashers and microwaves.
- Large freezers are not so common as shopping is often done on a daily basis.
- Kettles are not widely used – water is still boiled in pans.
- Most apartments have spacious balconies.

La terraza

For much of the year Spanish people can enjoy being outdoors. Outside the kitchen there is usually a patio *(terraza)* with a large table for family gatherings. Many have a barbecue or a gas paella ring. This has traditionally been the 'male' area – the men cook the paella or roast the meat.

Although the kitchen *(la cocina)* is central to Spanish life because so much time is devoted to preparing meals and eating with family and friends, they are not, as a rule, very large in apartments. This area belongs to the women of the house!

Traditional Spanish homes have a hallway *(un zaguán* or *un recibidor)* where visitors can be received. In smaller homes there is usually one large room which acts as a living room *(la sala)* and as a dining room *(el comedor)*. The table generally occupies centre stage, though the television is trying hard to take over. Spanish families sit around the table a lot – there is considerably less lounging around on large sofas!

Bedrooms *(una habitación* or *un dormitorio)* are usually kept quite apart from the rest of the house.

The Spanish are not really a nation of gardeners in the same sense as in the UK. More people live in flats in Spain than in the UK so do not have gardens. Outdoor space has typically been regarded as a place to grow food as a means of feeding the family, rather than as a place to have flowers and a lawn. However, there are balconies with pots of geraniums everywhere!

Read the information on pages 12 and 13 and complete the quiz.

1 What percentage of people live in rented accommodation in Spain? How does this compare with the UK?
2 Explain what a *'brasero'* is.
3 Give five differences between homes in Spain and the UK.
4 Use a dictionary and the words from pages 12 and 13 and describe your home in Spanish.
5 Do Spanish people have gardens? Explain your answer.

In Spain, there are many different types of house, depending on the region and the climate.

In Galicia, in northern Spain, traditional houses have wooden galleries *(galerías)* and enclosed glass balconies.

In the rural communities of Aragon, Catalonia and the Basque region, houses are traditionally rough stone constructions *(masías)*. They often have space for animals, tools and firewood on the ground floor with the family living area above. Some of the Basque houses look a little like the wooden chalets in Switzerland.

In Castilla-Leon, you might see a timber-framed house.

The thatched and whitewashed cottages of Valencia are known as *barracas*.

The whitewashed houses of the *pueblos blancos* of Andalusia are made of baked clay and have small windows and thick walls to keep the inside cool.

Cave houses

In the village of Guadix, near Granada in Andalusia, people have lived for centuries in about 2 000 caves carved into the hillside. The caves are cool in the summer and warm in the winter. Some are very spacious and have electricity, running water and even a television.

◀ In Cuenca, houses dating from the fourteenth century cling to the side of steep cliffs.

The **subsidised housing strategy** *(Vivienda de Protección Oficial)* took two forms: the *VPO de promoción Pública*, using government housing contractors, and the *VPO de promoción Privada*, using private developers.

Built-up residential areas dominated by tower blocks transformed the wastelands around cities. Even with subsidised housing it was not uncommon for families to have tenants living with them in order to make ends meet.

Social housing

When people left the countryside and migrated to towns during the fifties and sixties, Franco's regime developed a strategy called the *Plan Nacional de Vivienda* (National Housing Plan). Its aim was to build four million homes between 1961 and 1976 as a way of dealing with the problem.

It is estimated that during these years one in seven people migrated to urban areas and many of them did so without the guarantee of a house to live in. As a result, shanty houses *(chabolas)*, made out of any kind of material available, shot up around the outskirts of bigger towns and cities. These have gradually disappeared as families have been re-housed.

Squatters

The property boom of the late eighties transformed Spanish society every bit as much as the educational reforms of the early seventies, but, for many, affordable housing was still just a dream. Whole communities of squatters *(Okupas)* took over vacant properties in cities. The Socialist government responded with another housing strategy and successfully reduced the number of homeless people from 700000 in 1990 to 12000 in 1993.

So much English!

Holiday homes

Today, many rural houses are being bought up as weekend or holiday homes by city dwellers who want to escape the hustle and bustle and heat of the cities, or by foreigners in search of a different way of life.

Increasingly, it is common for British people to relocate to Spain. A popular area is Andalusia, where 50% more homes are being built than in Madrid or Barcelona. The influx of British settlers has reversed the migration effect of the fifties and sixties, with ghost towns in rural areas becoming repopulated, but the cost of housing has also increased.

Read the information on pages 14 and 15 and complete the quiz.

1 What are the features of houses in the south of Spain? Explain why.
2 What do you know about houses in Guadix?
3 Who are *Okupas*?
4 What does *VPO* stand for? Is there something similar in the UK?
5 Why are 50% more houses being built in Andalusia? Give details.
6 Explain the term 'migration effect'. Has there ever been anything similar in the UK?

4 School life

Compulsory school age

Spain	6 - 16
France	6 - 16
Germany	6 - 16
UK	5 - 16

Average hours at school per year

Average school days per year

Spain	170
France	180
Germany	188
UK	190

Average school holidays per year

Spain	18 weeks
France	16 weeks
Germany	14 weeks
UK	13 weeks

Spanish people value learning and consider education to be an essential way forward in life. It is said that the education reforms of the 1970s, 1990s and 2002 have done more to transform Spanish society than anything else.

From about the age of 3, many children go to a **crèche** *(una guardería infantil)* and at 4 or 5 years old they go to a **nursery school** *(un jardín de infancia* or *parvulario)*, especially in the larger towns and cities. At least 90% of 4- and 5-year-olds receive *educación preescolar*, as places are free in State nurseries. They can stay from 9am until 2pm *(media jornada)*, or until 4 or 5pm *(jornada completa)*, learning numbers, colours, how to read and how to write their names.

At 6 years old, children start compulsory education in **primary school** *(escuela primaria)* where they are taught by a class teacher *(un/a maestro/a)*. They also begin to learn a foreign language from the age of 8 in State schools. Class sizes are limited to twenty-five pupils.

Subjects at primary school

Lengua y literatura
Matemáticas
Conocimiento del medio
Educación artística
Educación física
Lengua extranjera
Religión

From the age of 12 to 16, pupils attend **secondary school** *(Centro de Educación Secundaria)*. They do not have assemblies, nor do they have to wear a uniform. Lessons start at around 9am and there is a half-hour break, usually from 11 to 11.30am. Pupils take a snack with them to eat or they can buy something from the canteen. Most pupils go home for lunch unless they have an extended day or live in a large city, in which case they would eat in the school canteen. Secondary schools finish at around 3pm. The *CCAA* sets the exact timing of the day for State schools, and many private schools have a long day – some don't finish until 5pm.

State secondary schools in Spain can be quite informal and contrast with the formality of private fee-paying schools where pupils usually wear a uniform.

Tronco común
(Core curriculum)

Lengua castellana y literatura
Lengua y literatura de la Comunidad Autónoma
Lengua extranjera
Matemáticas
Ciencias sociales, Geografía e Historia
Educación física
Ciencias de la naturaleza
Educación plástica y visual
Tecnología
Música
Religión/ética/actividades alternativas

Optativas

Segunda lengua extranjera
Procesos de Comunicación
Taller de Matemáticas
Taller de Artesanías

All schools have to follow a **national curriculum**. Most pupils (about 75%) go to a State school for all abilities and most schools are mixed. Class sizes are limited to 30 pupils. There are some private schools, which are usually run by the Catholic Church or, increasingly, by groups wanting to teach their own curriculum and culture as well as the national one.

The Ministry of Education makes the main laws regarding education; for example, it is now not compulsory to take religion, pupils can take ethics instead. However, the *CCAA* also share the responsibility of delivering free education for all and have some say in setting the curriculum. So, especially at secondary level, pupils will have different option choices depending on which region they live in. Some regional autonomies, such as Catalonia and the Basque region, teach in their own languages.

A new law *(la Ley Orgánica de Calidad)*, passed in December 2002, states that all autonomous regions have a district counselling team consisting of advisors for the curriculum, psychologists and social workers, and schools are required to offer guidance and support for Special Needs and Careers. However, many autonomies have been doing this for a long time already.

The school year runs from early September to the end of June but each autonomy sets its own specific dates.

In secondary school, pupils follow four years of compulsory education *(Educación Secundaria Obligatoria* or *ESO)*. During the first two years (for 12–14-year olds), all pupils study the same subjects *(asignaturas)* with one option choice.

Read the information on pages 16 and 17 and complete the quiz.

1. Where do children under the age of 6 go to school?
2. What is different about lunchtime at school in Spain and lunchtime in the UK?
3. Use your dictionary to write down the core subjects studied at secondary schools in Spain.
4. With a partner, list the main similarities and differences between schools in Spain and the UK.
5. How do the autonomous regions influence the curriculum? Do you think this is a good idea? What problems do you think this could cause?
6. What has the new Education Act of 2002 insisted upon?

Las optativas

These subjects must be offered:

- *Segunda lengua extranjera*
- *Cultura clásica*
- *Iniciación profesional*

These subjects may be offered:

- *Taller de astronomía*
- *Imagen y expresión*
- *Taller de teatro*
- *Canto coral*
- *Expresión corporal*
- *Transición a la vida adulta y activa*
- *Conservación y recuperación del patrimonio cultural*
- *Energías renovables y medio ambiente*
- *Botánica aplicada*
- *Papeles sociales de mujeres y hombres*
- *Informática*
- *Materias diseñadas por el Centro de educación*

UK	
11–12	Yr 7
12–13	Yr 8
13–14	Yr 9
14–15	Yr 10
15–16	Yr 11

Spain	
12–13	1° de Eso
13–14	2° de Eso
14–15	3° de Eso
15–16	4° de Eso

In the third year of secondary school, pupils continue with a set of core subjects *(el tronco común)* and also elect to take one different option *(una optativa)*. In the fourth year they can choose two different options. This is done in consultation with their parents and tutors.

Assessment

Pupils are assessed and graded regularly by their teachers through a series of tests *(una evaluación)* or on homework assignments. They are expected to pass in all subjects. If they fail a subject they have to retake *(revalidar)* and if they fail in several subjects at the end of the year they may be allowed to do a special resit *(un examen de reválida)* after the summer holidays. Sometimes pupils have to retake the whole year *(repetir)*.

Estoy en segundo de ESO.
Mis asignaturas preferidas son las ciencias y las matemáticas. Me encantan todos los deportes también.

Leaving school

At the end of the four years, all pupils receive a certificate stating the number of years studied and their grades. If they successfully reach all the grades for these four years they receive a Certificate in Education. If they don't achieve the grades they can go on to a Programme of Curricular Diversification, which gives them basic skills, or they can follow a Social Guarantee programme to help them gain basic and professional training to enable them to get a job.

Juan Carlos I, Rey de España

y en su nombre

La Consejera de Educación y Ciencia de la Junta de Andalucía

Considerando que, conforme a las disposiciones y circunstancias prevenidas por la legislación vigente,

ha superado los estudios regulados en los Reales Decretos 1007/1991, de 14 de junio y 894/1995, de 2 de junio y en los Decretos de la Junta de Andalucía 106/1992, de 9 de junio y 262/1996, de 28 de mayo, en el Instituto de Educación Secundaria "Salduba" de Marbella (Málaga), código 29011540, en junio de 2001, expide a su favor el presente

TÍTULO DE GRADUADA EN EDUCACIÓN SECUNDARIA

con carácter oficial y validez en todo el territorio español, que le faculta para ejercer los derechos que a este título otorgan las disposiciones vigentes.

Sevilla, a 13 de noviembre de 2001

La interesada, La Consejera de Educación y Ciencia, El Secretario General Técnico,

SERIE-JA. N° A-402354

Registro Autonómico de Títulos 010113069831

Post-16

In order to continue their education after the age of 16, pupils need the Certificate of Education to go onto a *Bachillerato* course. There are three types of *Bachillerato* – Arts; Science and Technology; Humanities and Social Studies, plus core subjects and options. Pupils have to pass the *Prueba General de Bachillerato* at the end of their two years of study. If they do not want to study an academic course then there is a Specific Vocational Training course *(Módulos de Formacíon Profesional)*. If they have the Certificate or pass a regional exam they can go straight onto the Intermediate level of Vocational Training. For the Advanced Vocational courses they need a *Bachillerato* and another regional-based exam. These courses are equivalent to EU Community Level 2 and 3 qualifications and have a lot of practical and work experience components.

University

Today, in Spain, more women than men go to university. To get in to university, students have to take an entrance exam *(un examen de selectividad)*. Often, degree courses *(la licenciatura)* are longer than in the UK – three years of core subjects *(communes)* and then specialisation. Young people often attend their local university and therefore carry on living at home for longer than most young people in the UK. If they want to study a specialised course away from home, they usually go to live in a Hall of Residence *(una residencia)*. Spain has an Open University *(Universidad a Distancia* or *UNED)*, where over 100 000 people, mostly over 30 years old, study.

▼ Salamanca university

The oldest university is in Salamanca, which was founded in 1218.

Read the information on pages 18 and 19 and complete the quiz.

1 What does *'revalidar'* mean? Does this happen in the UK?
2 Do you think the system of assessment is a good idea? Discuss.
3 What would be the Spanish equivalent of Year 9?
4 How many option choices are pupils allowed to take in Year 10? How does this compare with what happens where you live?
5 What does the term *'selectividad'* mean? Is there something similar in the UK?
6 What is the *UNED* in Spain? Name the UK equivalent.

5 Leisure

Football

Football is considered to be the national sport of Spain, attracting devoted fans. Every town has a football pitch and children usually learn to play as soon as they can walk. As in the UK football league, Spain boasts many foreign players – over 150 players in Division One. The season starts in September and finishes in June, with most matches taking place on Sundays. Just as in the UK, rivalry between top teams such as Barcelona and Madrid is intense. There are three magazines solely devoted to the football league.

La Liga: Barcelona, Real Madrid, Atlético Madrid, Deportivo, Valencia and Atlético Bilbao.

The stadiums in Spain are massive. Real Madrid's stadium, Santiago Bernabeu, holds up to 130 000 people, compared to Manchester United's ground at Old Trafford, which holds 60 000.

Young people in Spain have very similar hobbies and leisure activities to young people in the UK, France and Germany. During term time, they have a lot of homework so most activities take place at weekends and during the long school holidays *(las vacaciones)*.

Music *(la música)*

Spanish teenagers enjoy a wide variety of music, including rap, techno and rock. 43% of Spanish teenagers buy CDs and records at least once a month. How many Spanish popstars and bands can you name?

Cinema *(el cine)*

Going to the cinema is another popular pastime for Spanish teenagers and is the second most popular leisure activity after going to bars and cafés.

Television *(la televisión)*

Reality TV has become very popular in Spain. Indeed, *Operación Triunfo* was the original format for the UK's 'Fame Academy' and received 15 million viewers for its finale, which helped sell over 14 million CDs for the rising stars of the show. Spain also has its own version of 'Big Brother', 'Who wants to be a Millionaire?' and many other popular programmes.

Sports *(los deportes)*

In addition to the usual sporting actives such as football *(el fútbol)*, basketball *(el baloncesto)* and beach volley ball *(el voleiplaya)*, extreme sports such as roller blading *(el patinaje)*, BMXing, surfing *(el surf)* and snowboarding are also increasingly popular.

By way of contrast, most adults give their favourite pastimes as hunting and shooting *(la caza)*, fishing *(la pesca)*, boules *(petanca)*, socialising and gathering in cafes and bars *(la tertulia)* and taking part in the traditional *paseo* (walk up and down).

Paradores (meaning 'place to stay over') are high quality State-owned hotels. They were developed in the 1920s to attract foreign tourists and also to encourage Spaniards to explore their own country. Many are refurbished ancient monuments, such as the thirteenth-century convent in Merida.

Spain has something to offer all holidaymakers: beaches *(las playas)*, countryside *(el campo)* and mountains *(las montañas)*.

On Friday evenings and during the long, hot summer months, towns and cities are virtually empty as Spaniards pour out of them to go and enjoy the countryside.

Spain has an increasing number of innovative and exciting theme parks that attract both tourists and local people alike. Two particularly impressive parks are *Terra Mítica* near Benidorm, based on myths and legends of the Mediterranean, and *Port Aventura* near Barcelona, which is one of Europe's largest, based on exotic locations such as Mexico, China and Polynesia.

In spite of having so many wonderful holiday opportunities within Spain, Spaniards are increasingly taking to overseas travel, visiting countries such as Cuba, Egypt, Central and South America, and the UK.

All over Spain, in small villages and big cities, local festivals *(fiesta mayor)* are organised. One of the most spectacular is in Sitges, near Barcelona, on 25 August. Crowds of tourists and locals are wowed by firework-spitting dragons, human towers and an amazing evening firework display.

Tierra **Agua** **Aire**

Espeleogia	Puenting
Surf	Hípica
Bicicleta de montaña	Parapente
Piragüismo	Submarinismo
Wind-surf	Vela
Escalada	Vuelo con motor

Read the information on pages 20 and 21 and complete the quiz.

1 What are the similarities between football in the UK and Spain?

2 Use the Internet or library to find out more information about:

a Your favourite football team in Spain.

b How many British players play in the Spanish League *(La Liga)*.

3 Look at the box above. Translate the words and match them to an image. Which sport would you most like to try and why?

4 Find out some more information about each sport (what equipment you need, where in Spain you can do it, is it expensive?).

Sport in Spain

The Spanish are passionate about sport. If they aren't playing it, they love watching it, both on television and live. Major world sporting events (the football World Cup in 1982, the Barcelona Olympics in 1992, the World Athletics Championships in 2000, and the World Swimming Championships in 2003) have been held in Spain and helped to maintain Spain's enthusiasm for all sports.

Tennis

Since Miguel Santana's triumphs, tennis has enjoyed huge popularity and today Spain boasts many top-ranking players in both the men's and women's games:

Sergi Bruguera, Carlos Moya, Arantxa Sánchez-Vicario, Conchita Martínez

Today, Juan Carlos Ferrero is called 'the king of clay' and Rafael Nadal (right) is tipped to be a superstar of the future.

Did you know?

- During the Japan/Korea World Cup, a Spanish journalist paid $25 to adopt a Korean puppy and saved it from being the main course in a Korean restaurant. He named it *Camachín*, after the Spanish football team coach Antonio Camacho, and gave it to the team as their 2002 World Cup mascot.
- Pelota, played in the Basque region of northern Spain, is the fastest ball game in the world, with the ball travelling at speeds of 220 km/h.

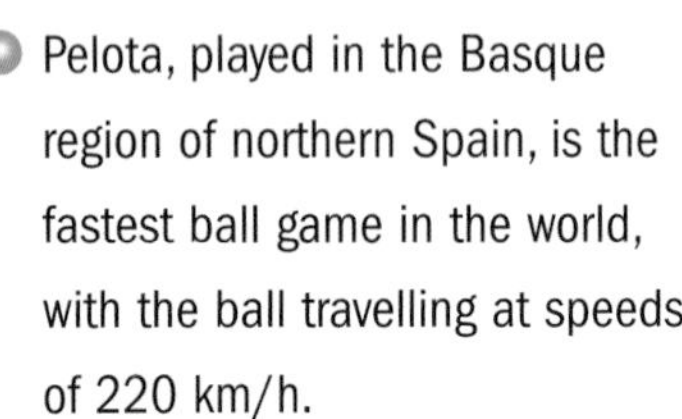

- Rafael Nadal is only the ninth player to win a professional tennis match before his sixteenth birthday.

Motor sport

Formula One is an increasingly popular spectator sport in Spain, mainly due to the emergence of a new Spanish talent, Fernando Alonso. He is just 22 years old and a champion in the making. Spain also has a strong motor sport tradition with names such as Carlos Sainz (rally driving), and Angel Nieto and Sete Gibernau (motor bike champions).

Golf

With an increasing demand from tourists, Spain now has over 150 golf courses, mainly concentrated in the southern regions of the Costa del Sol, now dubbed the 'Costa del Golf'. Spain ranks twelfth in the world for the highest number of courses. Like other sports, interest in the game has been helped by the success of players such as Sevi Ballesteros, José María Olazábal and now the young gun, Sergio García (ranked World number eight).

Pelota vasca

Pelota vasca, or *jai alai*, is an ancient sport played by the Basques from the sixteenth century onwards, and is still widely played in the north of Spain. The ball is thrown from a woven glove *(chistera)* against a concrete wall and travels at speeds of up to 220 km/h.

Cycling

Spain's success in professional cycling can be attributed to the brilliance of rider Miguel Induráin who won the Tour de France five times from 1991–1995. Spain has a number of leading teams, such as Banesto and ONCE. There are over 500 competitive races throughout the year. Other names to watch are Roberto Era and Oscar Sevilla.

Water sports

Water sports of all descriptions are hugely popular and competition sailing is a hobby of King Juan Carlos and Prince Felipe.

Athletics

Abel Antón (a marathon winner) and Fermín Cacho (the 1500 metre gold medallist at the Barcelona Olympics) have helped to boost the sporting prowess of young Spaniards.

Read the information on pages 22 and 23 and complete the quiz.

1. a Why are sports such as tennis, golf and motor racing so popular?
   b What is the regional sport of the Basque region?
2. Use the Internet or the library to find out more information about a tennis player from the box on page 22. Find out about his or her life and write a short biography.
3. Who is Spain's cycling hero and why?
4. Match up a sport in column A to a piece of equipment in column B.

A	B
fútbol	*palos*
tenis	*paracaidas*
golf	*botas*
pelota	*una bicicleta*
parapente	*un casco*
escalada	*una raqueta*
ciclismo	*una cordada*
fórmula uno	*una chistera*

6 Food and drink

Did you know?

- Mayonnaise was 'discovered' by the French at Mahon (Maó), the capital of Menorca, in the 1770s and they took the recipe back to France.
- The world's largest tortilla was made with 10 000 eggs, 1 200 kg of potatoes, 400 onions, 25 kg of salt and 200 litres of olive oil. It took a crane to turn it.
- Spain has over 4 500 different types of wine.
- Madrid has the world's second largest fish market.
- The average Spaniard consumes 10 litres of olive oil a year – the average northern European consumes one third of a litre.
- A third of Europe's olive oil is produced in Andalusia.

The Spanish love their food and spend a long time preparing and eating meals. Meal times are an important part of the day and are spent with family and friends.

The **Spanish diet** is considered to be a very healthy one – it includes lots of olive oil, garlic, fresh fruit, fish and, of course, red wine. Although many of the ingredients used in Spanish cooking are similar, different regions of the country have their own specialised and traditional ways of preparing dishes.

The Spanish do not usually have a large **breakfast** *(el desayuno)*. A normal breakfast might be just a coffee *(un café)* with or without milk *(con leche* or *solo)*, a juice *(zumo)*, and bread *(pan)* or croissants *(bollos)*. On special occasions, a popular breakfast for children is *chocolate con churros*, a doughnut dipped in thick, gooey hot chocolate (see page 9).

At school, for a **mid-morning snack**, children eat a roll *(bocadillo)* filled with ham *(jamón)*, cheese *(queso)* or sometimes even a slice of omelette *(tortilla)*.

Lunch *(el almuerzo* or *la comida)* is often eaten late, between 2 and 4pm. Some families still eat lunch together even on weekdays and for many this is the largest meal of the day.

Children have a **light snack** *(merienda)*, traditionally a chunk of plain chocolate and a glass of milk, when they get back from school at around 5pm.

After having a large meal at lunchtime, many people prefer to have a light **supper** *(la cena)* of salad *(una ensalada)* and cold meats *(embutidos)*, or maybe veal *(escalopa milanesa)* and mashed potato *(puré)*. This is often eaten very late at around 10 or 11pm.

At weekends, it is not unusual for families and friends to gather together for long, drawn-out lunches which can last for up to 5 or 6 hours.

Cafeteria sandwich

MIXTO especial €3,00
jamón, queso y cebolla

MARINO €3,50
ensaladillo, pepino y sardines

MANHATTAN €4,00
salmón, lechuga, huevo y mayonesa

VEGETAL CALIFORNIA €3,20
lechuga, huevo, tomate y queso

RURAL €3,60
pollo, bacon, tomate y lechuga

TRANVIA €4,30
bistec, cebolla, lechuga y tomate

Cafés, bars and restaurants

In Spain, it is possible to see people eating at cafés and restaurants throughout the day. Most bars and cafés serve cheap, but delicious, hot and cold snacks *(tapas)* and local dishes *(platos típicos)*. Restaurants provide very reasonable three-course daily set menus *(menu del día)* at lunchtime, with a choice of soups *(sopas)* and salads *(ensaladas)* followed by a meat or fish *(carne* or *pescado)* dish and finally a dessert *(postre)*, such as fresh fruit *(fruta fresca)* or flan *(crema catalana)*.

Fast food

The tradition of eating *tapas* and *churros* sitting at tables in the street or in bars has meant that fast food, as we know it in the UK, has not yet become widespread. However, increasingly, all over Spain, hamburgers *(hamburguesas)* and hot dogs *(perros calientes)* are very popular.

Chiringuitos, little kiosks on the beach, sell a variety of fresh fish and snacks and are very popular with Spaniards and tourists alike.

The tradition of *tapas* is thought to have originated from an old bar-room custom of putting bread over customers' drinks to keep flies out. The customers would then slowly nibble the bread while drinking. Over time, the bread became covered in other nibbles, such as cheese or olives. Tapas can be served on cocktail sticks *(pinchos)* or in larger portions ideal for sharing *(raciones)*, such as plates of grilled prawns *(gambas a la plancha)*, spicy sausage *(chorizo)*, or anchovies in garlic and oil *(boquerones)*.

Read the information on pages 24 and 25 then complete the quiz.

1 **a** Why is a Spanish diet considered healthy?
   b What are the similarities and differences between Spanish and British eating habits?
   c What are *tapas*?
2 Label the food in the shopping trolley on page 24.
3 Use a Spanish dictionary and make a list of food and drink you have for breakfast, lunch and dinner. Compare this with what a typical Spanish person might eat.
4 Language focus: look at the wordsearch and find 12 traditional Spanish foods or dishes (one is already done for you).

s b n e n s a l a d a f ñ m
a o a u í c h u l e t a s z
n l p h f e g d q é l l á c
g ñ a a c r s r z u m o g h
r x n w d v i ó r r f y s o
í a r c k e u n é t f c á r
a n é v ó z m j s o y a p i
á s b d e a ñ a w r j f k z
j t v s h q d p r t n é t o
r e j a m ó n g u i o c b j
c n r u v i n o e l s l ó m
é t h e u d t k o l y c l a
v o m y z ó b p l a i z o n
c r e m a c a t a l a n a s

Vegetarianism

Like many European countries, vegetarianism is on the increase in Spain but it is not as widespread as in the UK. When ordering food, be careful, as many traditional dishes such as omelettes contain small pieces of bacon or ham.

Spain's delicious, colourful range of food can be traced back to early Roman and Arab influences and the Spanish conquest in the Americas. The Romans bought grapes *(uvas)* and the Arabs bought new food such as rice *(arroz)*, which is still a staple ingredient. After returning from the Americas in the fifteenth century, the explorers brought back new food, yet to be seen in Europe, such as peppers *(pimientos)*, tomatoes *(tomates)*, potatoes *(patatas)*, sweetcorn *(maíz)* and, perhaps more importantly, chocolate *(chocolate)*.

The Arabs also introduced oranges *(naranjas)*; the word for orange comes from the Arabic *'naraj'*. The most famous orange-growing area is Seville, which produces the world-famous Seville orange – a large, bitter orange used to make marmalade. The Spanish for jam is *mermelada*, which is where the English word 'marmalade' originates. In the 1982 Fifa World Cup™, the Spanish mascot was a little orange called Naranjito.

► The Official Mascot of the 1982 Fifa World Cup™.

The olive tree was originally introduced to Spain by the Phoenicians and today Spain is the world's leading olive producer.

Drinks

Wine is drunk with most meals. One of the best known is Rioja, which is produced in the north of Spain and has an annual production of nearly 400 million bottles. In addition to wine, Spain is a leading producer and exporter of sherry *(jerez)*, a strong, fortified wine which is typically drunk before or after a meal.

Beers *(cervezas)*, such as San Miguel, Aguila and Cruz Campo, are of high quality and excellent value in Spain. They are now also sold in many bars in the UK.

Coffee culture

The Spanish are a nation of coffee lovers and they drink it in many forms – black *(solo)*, with a drop of milk *(cortado)* or white *(café con leche)*. These are served in a variety of permutations – the best being a *carajillo* (a *café solo* with a shot of brandy), which is a good pick-me-up or after-meal drink.

Spanish drinks

Sangría – a mix of wine, fruit and soda water, with a drop of brandy

Horchata de chufas – a milky nut drink

Batido de leche – milkshake

Cava – sparkling wine made like champagne (but cheaper!)

Regional dishes

Central Spain is known for its wonderful game – partridge, pheasant and wild boar. A typical dish is *perdiz con chocolate* – braised partridge with carrots and onions covered in a chocolate-flavoured gravy! *Queso manchego*, Spain's best-known cheese, is produced in La Mancha.

Northern Spain – miles of Atlantic coastline mean fish dishes such as *bacalao al pilpil* are typical of Northern Spain, as well as dishes such as pork stew *(fabada asturiana)* made from beans, sausages and other pork meat.

Eastern Spain – Valencia is a major rice-producing region and gives its name to the *paella valenciana*, a delicious mix of saffron rice, rabbit, chicken or pork, and peppers. This hearty meal was originally made by the farm workers out in the fields and is best cooked over a large wood fire. Today, it has many variations to suit tourist tastes – a favourite being seafood paella.

Southern Spain – *gazpacho*, originally from Andalusia, is a cold soup made mainly from tomatoes and peppers and usually served with diced onions and croutons (fried bread cubes). Some of the finest cured hams *(jamón serrano)* come from Andalusia.

Read the information on pages 26 and 27 and complete the quiz.

1 a What influence did the Arabs and Romans have on Spanish cuisine?
  b What food was discovered in the Americas?
  c What is the significance of the orange?
  d What is special about Jerez? Look for the town on a map.
  e Which region is famous for its rice dishes?

2 Which of the dishes would you like to try and why?

3 Make a list of traditional food and drink in the UK and put them in order of preference. Describe one of them in Spanish to a partner and see if he or she can guess which it is.

4 Use the Internet or library and find a recipe for one of the dishes mentioned on page 27. Explain to your partner what the key ingredients are and how to prepare it.

7 Festivals and traditions

It is certainly true that the Spanish know how to party and enjoy themselves. This is reflected in the fact that Spain has over 3000 festivals and fiestas each year, combining music, dancing, costumes and processions.

January | February | March | April | May | June | July | August | September | October | November | December

6 January

El Día de los Reyes – Feast of Kings (Epiphany)

19 March

Las Fallas – St Joseph's day

Huge papier-maché monuments *(fallas)* are set up in squares and streets all over Valencia on 19 March.

23 April

El Día del Libro – Cervantes day

15 May

San Isidro

This Madrid festival is in honour of Saint Isidore, the capital's patron saint.

24 June

San Juan

7–14 July

Fiesta de San Fermín

end of August

La tomatina

On the last Wednesday in August, the town of Bunyol in Valencia hosts a tomato battle.

12 October

El Día de la Hispanidad (see Chapter 1)

Spain's national holiday

Turrón is a sticky, sweet nougat made of almonds and honey. It is a favourite at Christmas time.

Spain has many religious festivals and holidays, especially over Christmas *(Navidad)* and Easter *(Semana Santa)*.

Over **Christmas** and **New Year** *(Año Nuevo)*, in every town and village there will usually be a crib *(belén)*, a Christmas tree *(árbol de navidad)* and lots of lights. Christmas dinner of roast turkey *(pavo asado)* is usually eaten on Christmas Eve *(Nochebuena)*, after which families go to midnight mass *(misa del gallo)* and sing Christmas carols *(villancicos)*.

On **New Year's Eve** *(Nochevieja)*, people see in the New Year by eating twelve grapes on each of the twelve chimes of midnight to bring them good luck. In Madrid, crowds meet in the main square of the Puerta del Sol to wish each other Happy New Year *(Feliz Año Nuevo)*.

The Three Kings *(Los Reyes Magos)* bring Spanish children their presents on 6 January.

An Easter procession

At Easter, processions of floats *(pasos)* carrying statues of the Virgin are followed by brotherhoods *(cofradías)* of people in white robes. The one in Seville is the most famous of the many Easter celebrations.

Corpus Christi is a colourful festival, with carpets of flowers covering the streets, to celebrate the patron saint of the town.

There is a different **Saint's Day** for every day of the year. Traditionally, Spanish people celebrate on the day whose saint's name they share.

Read the information on pages 28 and 29 and complete the quiz.

1 Find out some more about the two festivals: *San Juan* and *San Fermín*. Tell a partner what you discovered about the festivals.

2 Use the information on page 29 to translate the following words into Spanish and complete the Christmas wordsearch (one is done for you): crib, Christmas tree, Christmas Eve, roast turkey, sticky nougat, Christmas carols, The Three Kings, New Year's Eve, Happy New Year.

3 Write a paragraph in English, summarising the similarities and differences between Spanish festivals and those held in the UK.

l b n o c h e b u e n a p y
c o u y o w c p d l o x a m
ñ k s k t u r r ó n c i v g
o a á r a í a s n r h q o ñ
z é s g e s l ó h n e f a í
t b d s v y ñ j w d v e s z
á r b o l d e n a v i d a d
l n e d i t k s c g e j d n
c e l j ó e á i m r j h o s
r l é t a x c n l a a r r a
u l n p f m h f e t g y n n
m p e v j é ó p á v m o h t
i b v i l l a n c i c o s o
f e l i z a ñ o n u e v o s

Tourist traditions

Two traditions that tourists often associate with Spain are flamenco and bullfighting. However, this is in fact a false perception of Spain.

Flamenco

Flamenco's origins are not easy to pinpoint but it has clear North African influences. Developed by the gypsies in the eighteenth century, it centred around Seville and Cadiz. It is a mixture of rhythms and music from the guitar, handclapping, castanets, singing and dancing. Flamenco has recently been exported to the world by the fiery dancer Joaquin Cortés and groups such as Paco Pena. The singers of the true *'cante jondo'* express the sorrows and joys of life in a unique style which is more profound and serious.

Bullfighting

Many of Spain's festivals centre around bulls, and the bullfight itself is known as the *Fiesta Nacional*. The bullfighting season lasts from March to October, with main fights taking place on Sundays. There are about 500 bullfighting rings in Spain – the biggest is in Madrid, which holds about 25 000 people.

Although bullfighting is clearly an important cultural tradition and certainly does have a large following, its popularity is not as widespread as people outside Spain believe. The anti-bullfight campaigners protest against the cruelty and barbarity of the 'sport'. Their protests have had some success in changing public opinion, resulting in the banning of bullfighting in a few mainland towns and the Canary Islands. It has also succeeded in the closure of a bullring in Barcelona. A more recent law has made it illegal for children under 14 to attend fights.

Today's star of bullfighting is **Francisco Rivera Ordóñez** – one of Spain's richest and most famous bullfighters. He is only 26 years old and comes from a family of bullfighting greats.

El Juli is another top bullfighter, who can command up to £80 000 per appearance. He fights up to 106 times a season and also has lucrative sponsorship deals with car and beer companies.

Romerías, when whole villages turn out for a mass pilgrimage to a rural shrine, are often accompanied by a picnic.

One of the great things about Spain is that even in modern times it has kept many of its oldest traditions alive and they are enjoyed by people of all generations. Every region has its own costume and folk dance, such as *Sevillanas* and *Jotas*.

▲ *Sardanas*. People hold hands in a circle and perform a complex combination of short steps, skips and jumps accompanied by an 11-piece band *(cobla)*, which consists of a flute *(flabiol)*, drum *(tabal)*, woodwind and brass instruments. It is performed on Sundays and at traditional festivals.

◀ National costumes are worn with pride during fiesta time. These women are enjoying themselves in Estepona at their *Fiesta Mayor* between 1 and 6 July.

Superstitions

- *Martes 13*
- Black cats are unlucky.
- Don't put flowers or hats on a bed.
- Take *'sal, aceite y carbón'* when you go to someone's new house.

Lotería Nacional

The Spanish are the biggest gamblers in Europe and the third biggest in the world after America and the Philippines. Every year, just before Christmas, on 22 December, Spain holds the world's biggest prize draw of a State lottery – *El Gordo* ('The Fat One'). The Spanish consider this to be the start of Christmas celebrations. It is possible to start buying tickets as early as August and as the day gets closer it is often difficult to buy tickets.

Read the information on pages 30 and 31 and complete the quiz.

1 a Why do you think bullfighters are treated like sport stars?
  b What are the origins of flamenco?
  c Name some typical Spanish superstitions. How are they similar or different to those in the UK?

2 Using the Internet or the library, find out about Spanish dances such as *'Pasadobles'* and *'Sevillanas'*. Write about the music, dances and costumes.

3 Write a paragraph on one of the following issues:
  a What traditions do you associate with the UK? Compare your ideas with a partner. Did you think of the same traditions?
  b Do you think bullfighting is a tradition that should be preserved or just a cruel sport that should be banned?
  c Is it important for each region to keep its own traditions? What are the arguments for and against?

8 Geography

The word *sierra* in Spanish means 'saw'.

Spain – the Peninsula

Spain is the last outpost of Europe, hidden away behind the Pyrenees. It was once joined to Africa, before the straits of Gibraltar evolved. Its capital city, Madrid, occupies centre stage at 660 metres above sea level and is one of the highest capitals in Europe (see Chapter 12).

With an incredibly varied landscape and climate, Spain is home to Europe's southern-most glacier and also some of Europe's only deserts. A series of mountain ranges *(sierras)* divide the country, helping to separate out the different regions. Much of central Spain is on a high, dry plateau called the *meseta*. Many of Spain's major **rivers** originate from here: the four main ones are the Tajo (1 007 km), the Ebro (910 km), the Duero (765 km) and the Guadalquivir (670 km).

The **Sierra Nevada** is the highest mountain range in Spain, of which the highest peak is the Pico de Mulhacén at 3 482 metres. The highest peak of the Spanish territory is Mount Teide at 3 718 metres on Tenerife.

The weather

In most of the country the summers are very hot. The north and central regions have freezing winters but in the south and east the winters are mild. The northern part of the country (Galicia, Cantabria and the Basque country) is very wet, while the southern parts of Spain suffer from lack of rainfall and droughts.

Paisajes Naturales

El torcal de Antequera

Located in Andalusia, in the south of Spain, these huge limestone rocks, carved out by thousands of years of rain and wind, are perhaps Spain's most spectacular natural sight.

Garganta del Chorro

This 180-metre-deep gorge has been carved out of the limestone mountain by the river Guadalhorce in Andalusia.

Picos de Europa

Christened 'the Peaks of Europe' by returning sailors who could see them from miles away, this amazing mountain range in the north of Spain is Europe's largest national park. It crosses three regions – Asturias, Cantabria and Castilla-Leon.

Cañadas de Teide

This huge crater, with a circumference of 80 km and an altitude of 2 000 metres, towers over the island of Tenerife. Piles of coloured lava and ash cover the landscape.

Read the information on pages 32 and 33 and complete the quiz.

1. a What geographical features divide mainland Spain?
   b How does the climate vary in different parts of the country?
   c Why do the geographical features of Spain make it such a unique country?
2. Find eight words that refer to geography and landscape (e.g. mountain). Use your dictionary to find the Spanish names for these features.
3. Imagine you are writing an article for a Spanish tourist brochure. Choose one of the places mentioned and write a short article. Read your article to a partner.

El Penyal de Ifach – Calpe

The Penyal de Ifach is one of the Costa Blanca's most dramatic sights, which was privately owned until 1987. It rises 332 metres and is now a nature reserve.

Amazing Andalusia

Andalusia is the largest *CCAA* in southern Spain and has everything – sun, sea, mountains and monuments. Its soul is the Guadalquivir – in Arabic 'the Great River' (Guad-al-Quivir). Andalusia is home to much of Spain's rich cultural history. Granada and Cordoba contain amazing examples of Moorish architecture, art and technological achievements.

The Alhambra palace in Granada is a masterpiece of Moorish architecture.

Andalusia is the most heavily populated region in Spain, with an estimated 7.357 million inhabitants, which is over 15% of the Spanish population. The major cities are Seville, Granada, Cordoba and Cadiz, although the busy tourist resorts of Malaga, Marbella and Torremolinos are probably more familiar.

The coastal regions of the Costa del Sol and the Costa de la Luz have an average of 300 days sunshine a year, making it a package-holiday heaven. Marbella is the most stylish and trendy resort, attracting the rich and famous to its luxury accommodation, 29 beaches and range of world-class leisure activities, especially the golf clubs.

Doñana National Park *(Parque Nacional de Doñana)* is 185 000 hectares in size and contains three types of eco-systems: marsh lands, wet lands and beaches. It is home to some very rare flowers, plants and animals, including the Spanish lynx, deer and the imperial eagle.

Andalusia's main industries are fishing, olive production and tourism (see Chapter 18).

Djebel Tarik (Tarik's mountain)

What a lot of fuss over 6 square kilometres of rock!

The 'rock' of Gibraltar was ceded to England in 1713 at the Treaty of Utrecht and has remained a sensitive issue ever since. It is home to around 40 000 people. Five million tourists a year visit the British colony to take advantage of the excellent tax-free shopping.

Away from the crowds in Mallorca

The islands

As well as the mainland, Spain also includes the Balearic Islands, the Canary Islands and two North African territories.

The Balearic Islands (Menorca, Mallorca, Formentera, Cabrera and the party island of Ibiza) are thriving tourist destinations famous for their landscapes, beaches and climate. They have been fought over and colonised throughout their early history by Phoenecians, Greeks, Carthaginians, Romans, Moors and Turks. All have left their mark, especially the last settlers, the Catalans, whose language formed the dialect spoken today. Palma de Mallorca is the capital of the archipelago and is home to one of the most important ports in the Mediterranean, as well as Spain's busiest airport.

Lanzarote's lunar landscape

The Canary Islands consist of seven islands and several more islets. They are very close to Western Morocco (but 1500 km from the Spanish mainland) and are very popular winter sunshine destinations. These islands were formed when hundreds of volcanoes erupted from the sea millions of years ago. They have amazing geographical features – lava deserts, primeval forests, a splendid variety of flora and fauna and, of course, wonderful sand dunes and beaches.

The other territories

The Spanish territories of Ceuta and Melilla, plus a few uninhabited islands on the north African coast of Morocco, have been held by Spain since the fifteenth century. Not unreasonably, they are claimed by Morocco but, in fact, Ceuta is governed by Cadiz, and Melilla is governed by Malaga. Ceuta boasts an old fortress, a large plaza and a cathedral but, like Gibraltar, it is perhaps better known for its tax-free shopping. Although Melilla is essentially a modern city, it too has preserved some of its historic sites.

Read the information on pages 34 and 35 and complete the quiz.

1 a Why is Andalusia a unique region?
  b What is the main industry on the Costa del Sol?
  c Why is Gibraltar a 'sensitive' issue for the Spanish government?
  d Which islands are Spanish territories?

2 Use the Internet or library and find out five interesting pieces of information about any of Spain's islands and report back to a partner.

3 Which region or city in Spain would you most like to visit and why?

4 Should countries hold on to historical outposts which naturally form part of another country? Discuss.

9 The people of Spain

The Romans called Spain *'Hispania'* – 'land of the rabbits' – because they were surprised by the vast number of rabbits they saw there!

Arabic words are often associated with the house and home life. They usually start with 'al' or 'ar'.

- *alcoba* – bedroom
- *alfombra*
- *arroz*
- *azúcar*
- *alcázar*

Spanish people are fiercely regionalistic – they nearly always defend their region before their country. The division of Spain into different regions is not just a result of physical geography and politics, but also of history. The various peoples who came and settled in Spain, from the earliest tribe, called the Ibers (who crossed over from north Africa and gave the name 'Iberia' to the land), to the Romans and Moors, have all left their mark on the Spanish language, culture and heritage. The wide range of physical and genetic makeup reflects this, as well as the regional music, costumes and traditions, which are still kept very much alive (see Chapter 7), and, of course, the different languages which are still spoken today (see Chapter 1).

Asturias and Cantabria
Basque Country
Navarra and La Rioja
Galicia
Castilla-León
Aragón
Catalonia
Madrid
Extremadura
Castilla-La Mancha
Balearic Islands
Andalusia
Murcia and Valencia

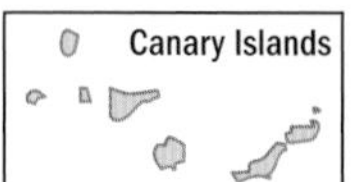

The **Basques** are one of the oldest races in Europe and speak a language unlike any other in the world. They are typically a short, dark-haired race. Sadly, today they are better known for their fight for total independence from Spain and their terrorist movement ETA *(Euskadi ta Azkatasuna* – homeland and freedom). They also have two provinces in France.

The **Galicians** *(gallegos)* inhabit the north-west corner of the country (Galicia) and are more akin to the Celtic tribes who invaded Spain. Their language and especially their music, with its bagpipes *(gaitas)* and drums *(tambores)*, resembles that of other Celtic peoples.

► Bagpipes and drums in Galicia

The people of **Catalonia** (*Cataluña* in Spanish, *Catalunya* in Catalan) have a long and proud history of independence. It is often said that they have more in common with the people of the south of France than with the rest of Spain. During the twelfth to fourteenth centuries, the Catalans ruled over a large area which included not only Corsica and Sardinia but also Athens (see left).

Throughout history, there has always been a strong rivalry between Barcelona and Madrid. Under Franco, who kept Madrid as the capital, this rivalry was made worse because he did his best to wipe out the Catalan language and culture, burning whole libraries of books and forbidding people to speak their language or sing their own national anthem. He did the same with the Basques. Naturally, there was a great deal of opposition from both groups to the dictatorship but the Catalans were never as fervent or violent in their nationalism as the Basques.

Today, the Catalan language and culture thrives. Catalan is taught in schools and has its own newspaper *(Aviu)*, as well as radio and television stations.

¿Parla català?

Catalan is spoken by nearly seven million people, which makes it more widely spoken than Danish and Norwegian.

It is spoken throughout the Balearic Islands and parts of northern Valencia, as well as Andorra, and an area of France called Roussillon. It is also spoken in Alguer, a walled town on the west coast of Sardinia. Until the 1950s it could still be heard in San Agustín, Florida, a town captured and inhabited by the Menorcans in the eighteenth century.

► *Castellers*, or human towers, up to seven people high are topped by a small child – *anxaneta*.

Read the information on pages 36 and 37 and complete the quiz.

1 What three factors helped to shape the regions of Spain?
2 How did the peninsula get its name?
3 What is special about the Basque language?
4 Look at the box of words on page 36 again. How many words do you know of Arabic origin? Can you add any more to the list?
5 How many people speak Catalan?
6 On a map, find the areas where Catalan is spoken.

4 000 Basque refugee children came to the UK in 1937.

Throughout its history, Spain has not only 'gained' people but has also 'lost' them. In 1492, Spain finally took back Granada and expelled the Moors. They also expelled the Jews who did not want to convert to Christianity.

Emigration

After the discovery of the Americas in 1492, many Spaniards went to the New World to seek their fortune or simply in the hope of a better life. This emigration continued for many centuries.

The Civil War (1936–1939) caused many thousands to flee Spain; some never returned, preferring voluntary exile to a dictatorship. Some have lived to return home but only after the death of Franco and the restoration of democracy.

Migration

During the 1960s, many Spanish people, especially from Andalusia and the poorer regions of Spain, migrated to the north, mainly to Barcelona, looking for work in the textiles and light industries. Many were also encouraged to go abroad and were even paid by the government to do so.

Immigration

During the last twenty years or so, many South and Central Americans *(americanos)* have returned to Spain, some as a result of persecution and others seeking a better life. In March 2002, the government brought out a new law requiring some of them (Colombians and Ecuadorians) to have a visa to enter Spain. This seems strange to them as they consider Spain to be their mother country.

6 EL DEBATE DE LA INMIGRACIÓN — EL PAÍS, DOMINGO 9 DE NOVIEMBRE DE 2003

El naufragio del 25 de octubre en el Estrecho, con un saldo de 45 muertos y desaparecidos, es, por ahora, la mayor tragedia de la inmigración clandestina. Un experto español, Pablo Pumares, y otro marroquí, Mehdi Lahlou, que han trabajado juntos por encargo de la OIT, opinan sobre el drama de la inmigración

¿Se pueden parar las pateras?

IGNACIO CEMBRERO

Cuando falta exactamente un mes para que una visita a Marruecos del presidente José María Aznar selle la normalización hispano-marroquí, iniciada en enero pasado tras 15 meses de larga crisis diplomática, el contencioso sobre la inmigración se ha convertido en el principal escollo para una plena reconciliación.

En octubre ha llegado a las costas andaluzas y canarias una avalancha sin precedentes de pateras en otoño. Hace dos semanas tuvo lugar la mayor tragedia de la inmigración clandestina cuando zozobró una *zodiac* con 50 pasajeros a bordo. En el naufragio, a 200 metros de la costa gaditana, murieron, presumiblemente, 45 marroquíes. Hubo cinco supervivientes.

Peor aún que esta oleada otoñal de inmigrantes es, desde el punto de vista del Ministerio del Interior español, la negativa de Rabat a readmitir a los subsaharianos que, procedentes de la costa de Marruecos, desembarcan en España. Además, los menores marroquíes, que han llegado a España en proporciones inusuales, son readmitidos por Rabat con cuentagotas, según denuncia Ignacio González, el delegado del

Una patrullera del servicio marítimo de la Guardia Civil, con un grupo de inmigrantes tras haber sido interceptadas dos pateras. EFE

Immigrant workers also come from North Africa, especially Morocco. They risk their lives crossing the straits of Gibraltar in small boats or rafts (called *pateras*). Some even swim across. Each week, several bodies are found on the beaches of Tarifa. In 1999, the Spanish government signed an agreement with Morocco to arrange for thousands of Moroccans to come over for nine months of the year to try to stem the flow of 'illegals' *(ilegales)*, as they are known. Morocco was once a Spanish colony so most speak basic Spanish.

Fería in Seville

Gypsies

Gypsies in Spain have always been kept on the fringe of society. They are typically dark-haired, dark-skinned people who have lived mainly in Andalusia for many centuries. They have a distinct language and traditions of their own and have tended to live on the edge of towns and cities. They have had rough treatment throughout their history. Their flamenco, singing, dancing and guitar playing has made them famous. Today, they are more integrated in to Spanish society and are gradually becoming more prosperous, in part thanks to the tourist invasion of the Costa del Sol.

Foreign tourists in Spain

- UK – 14 million
- Germany – 10.5 million
- France – 6.7 million
- Italy – 2.2 million
- Holland – 2.2 million
- Belgium – 1.6 million
- Portugal – 1.4 million

Tourists

One final group to consider when talking about the people of Spain are the tourists who visit for long periods of time, or foreigners who have stayed and made their home there. It is hard to put a figure on this fluctuating population but estimates range from 4 to 5 million.

What do the Spanish think about this? On the one hand, they are pleased because it brings in trade and boosts the economy. On the other hand, the older generation, in particular, finds it hard because they feel that the foreigners tend to create little societies of their own and do not integrate or try to learn the language.

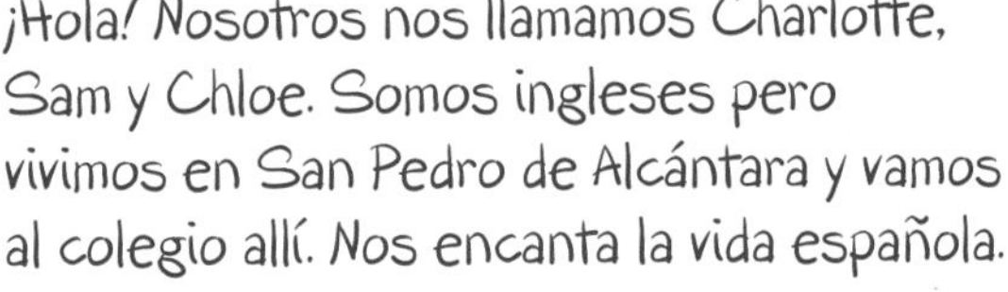

Read the information on pages 38 and 39 and complete the quiz.

1. Explain what you think is meant by 'gain' and 'lose' people?
2. Why is 1492 such an important date in Spanish history?
3. How did the Civil War affect the people of Spain?
4. How are people from Morocco treated?
5. Would you like to live in Spain? Would you find it hard to adapt to life there? Why? What would you miss most?

10 In the country

Rural contrasts

Country life has changed far less in Spain than city life and many villages look as though time has stood still. Most rural people still work on the land and continue in their time-honoured traditions and customs. However, some coastal resort areas have changed beyond all recognition due to the influx of tourists.

Since Spain joined the European Union in 1986, artificial pesticides and fertilizers have been introduced, as well as huge machines. Refineries and chemical works are becoming more and more evident, which increases the problem of pollution.

In addition, the growth of tourism is having a dual impact on rural life. On the one hand, it brings development and much-needed prosperity, but, on the other hand, it can ruin the natural surroundings. The government is keen to develop rural tourism given that many tourists have tired of the *costas* and want to seek out more of the 'real' Spain.

The property boom of the late 1980s onwards is taking its toll on vast areas of the countryside, which are being devastated in the name of progress. Developers gouge out huge areas of unspoilt countryside to create theme parks and golf courses, build mock villages clinging to hillsides, or leave behind them huge swathes of concrete high-rises on the coast.

Endangered species in Spain

- Bear
- Lynx
- Imperial eagle

Spain has a unique flora and fauna and most of Spain remains a haven for wildlife. 10% of the 8 000 species of flora found in Spain are found nowhere else in the world. Spain is still one of the best places to go bird watching.

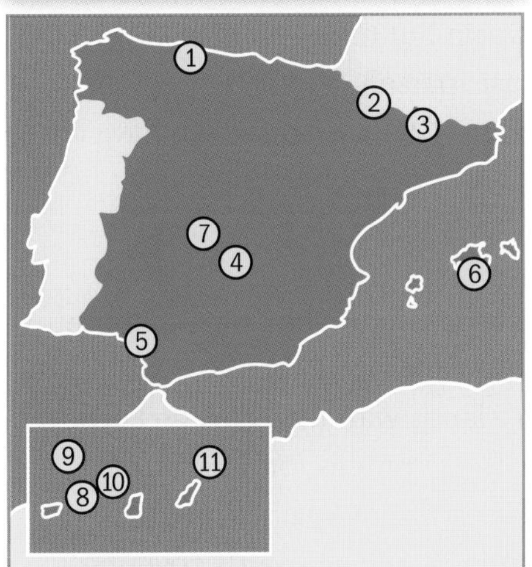

1. Picos de Europa
2. Ordesa y Monte Perdido
3. Aigues Tortes y el lago de Sant Maurici
4. Tablas de Daimiel
5. Doñana
6. Archipiélago de Cabrera
7. Cabañeros
8. Garajonnay
9. Caldera de Taburiente
10. Teide
11. Timanfaya

Environmental issues

The average Spaniard has recently become much more aware of and sensitive to environmental issues. Today, there are several important groups working to raise awareness, and schools have environmental studies as part of the curriculum. Most towns have recycling bins.

The *Instituto para la Conservación de la Naturaleza (ICONA)* monitors environmental issues. Increasingly, people are protesting about developments that they feel are harmful to the environment, one such example is the Somport tunnel through the Pyrenees, which opened in 2003.

Spain was one of the first nations to establish nature reserves and created a series of national parks in 1918. Two people, Dr Felix Rodríguez de la Fuente and José Antonio Valverde, have been key figures in raising public awareness about conservation issues. Spain has eleven national parks (see left) and over 200 regional parks and nature reserves, covering about 1 226 km^2.

Spain has suffered several devastating chemical and oil spillages in the Coto Doñana National Park in 1998 and more recently in November 2002, when the Prestige ran aground off the Galician coast.

Read the information on pages 40 and 41 and complete the quiz.

1. What changes have taken place in the countryside?
2. How many species of flower are there in Spain?
3. Use your dictionary to write down, in Spanish, the endangered species of Spain. Do we have any endangered species in the UK? Write their names in Spanish.
4. What environmental groups are there in Spain? What groups are there in the UK? Do you think it is important to belong to one?
5. What ideas do you have for local environmental projects?

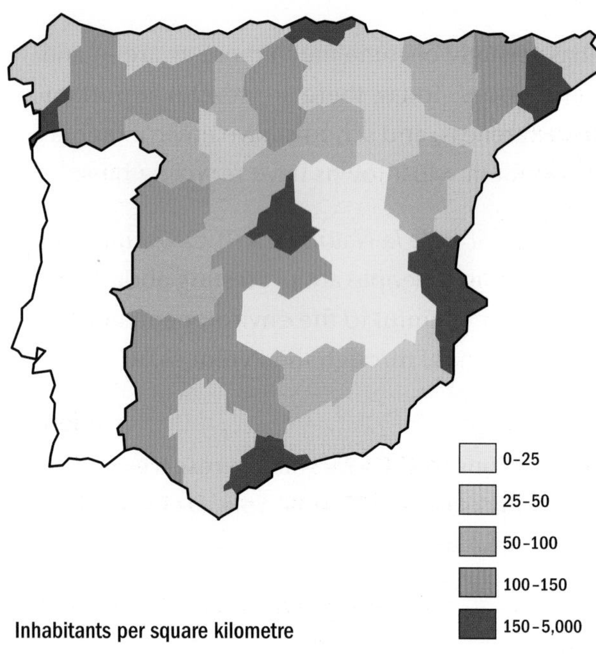

Inhabitants per square kilometre

Population

Spain has a vast open countryside that is sparsely populated. During the 1960s and 1970s, whole villages were deserted as young people, in particular, left the country to look for work in cities and towns. However, many Spanish families have held on to their roots in the country and have kept up a second home there as an escape from city life. The average population density is about 80 inhabitants per square kilometre, one of the lowest levels in Europe, but this varies enormously from region to region. Some of the regions, such as Extremadura, Castilla-La Mancha, Castilla-Leon, Aragon and Navarra, make up half the total land mass of Spain but have less than 16% of the population. The most sparsely populated regions of all are Soria, Teruel and Guadalajara, which have an average of 12 inhabitants per square kilometre.

Population density per km^2

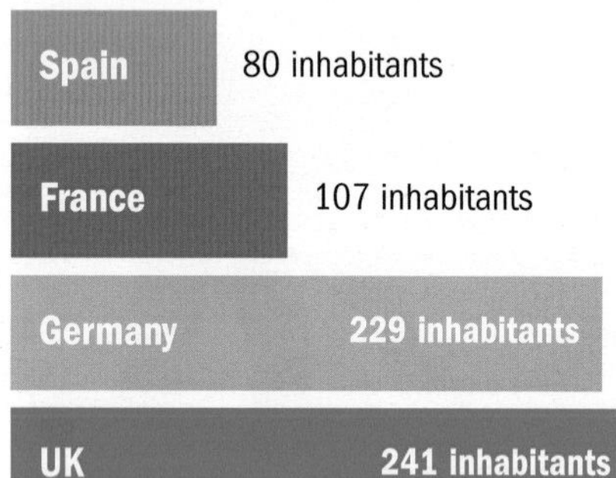

Land

Spain has an enviable variety of landscapes. In the north-west, there are the fjords of Galicia, called the *rías*, while along the coast of the Bay of Biscay there are green, lush pasture lands with the Picos de Europa rising high above them. To the north, the Pyrenees form a natural barrier between France and Spain. The centre of Spain is one large plateau or *meseta* with extensive cornfields and vineyards covering over 200 000 km^2. In the south, towards Andalusia, are the most exotic looking olive groves, and, to a lesser extent, orange groves, while in the east, there are the fertile *huertas* (orchards) of Valencia. Half of the soil in Spain is unproductive and barren, and some parts of the south-east are almost desert-like, providing the perfect location for the many spaghetti westerns filmed there.

Bilbao
Barcelona
MADRID
Valencia
Seville

vineyards
wheat
olive groves
sheep farming
oranges and lemons
rice
dairy farming

Villages

Villages in Spain tend to be grouped around the church, which occupies the highest point. Streets are narrow, often with rough cobblestones, and usually lead to a central square where, traditionally, people come out and sit in the cool of the evening. In past times, there would always have been a water fountain.

In the north and north-east, you can still see isolated farm houses *(masías)* tucked away in the folds of the hills and mountains (see Chapter 3).

Hórreo – a grain store in Asturias

In Asturias, people still use *hórreos* – square wooden store houses with tiled roofs, perched on top of 'stilts' to prevent rats reaching the grain and food stored in them.

In central Spain, on the vast plains of Castille, villages are grouped together, sometimes even walled in. One particularly striking feature is the number of storks nesting on the rooftops or trees, and the windmills.

On the eastern edges of the *meseta*, towards Valencia and Alicante, is the most incredible looking village, with houses that cling to the sides of rocky outcrops. These are known as the *casas colgantes de Cuenca* (see page 14).

The villages of the south are the typical picture postcard white villages perched on top of hills, known as the *pueblos blancos de Andalucía*.

A few people still live in caves albeit with all mod cons (see Chapter 3), though this is very exceptional!

Read the information on pages 42 and 43 and complete the quiz.

1 What are the least populated areas in Spain? What are the least populated areas in the UK?
2 Why do so many Spanish people have a second home?
3 What are the main farming areas of Spain? What do they produce?
4 What are the main features of a typical Spanish village? Compare this with a typical village in the UK.
5 Where would you prefer to live – town or country? Explain your reasons.

11 In town

Casco viejo – the old quarter

Much of Spain's population is concentrated around the coastal areas, with the obvious exception of the capital, Madrid. In fact, Madrid and Barcelona account for over 25% of the total population and about 75% of Spaniards live in towns of over 10000 inhabitants.

A typical Spanish town will usually have an **old quarter** *(el barrio antiguo* or *el casco viejo)*, which will be centred around the most important buildings – the town hall *(el ayuntamiento)*, the castle *(el castillo)*, and the church *(la iglesia)* or cathedral *(la catedral)*. Inevitably, there will be various squares *(plazas)* and, more often than not, a main square *(Plaza Mayor)*.

The **market** *(el mercado)* is an important feature in any Spanish town. Some only provide fresh fruit and vegetables but many have an interesting array of wares and even livestock. Spanish people love market day and always choose to buy fresh produce there whenever they can. Recently, the Boquería market in Barcelona was voted the best in the world by a British newspaper.

► The Boquería market in Barcelona

In Spain, refuse is collected regularly – daily in some large towns. The streets are also hosed down in the early morning.

Today, you will find Internet cafés in most towns, which also have telephone booths so you can make cheap long-distance calls.

Spanish people are a nation of shopaholics. Shops *(las tiendas)* in Spain vary widely from **large stores** *(almacenes)* in the high streets to big, out-of-town **shopping centres** *(zonas commerciales)*. Many shopping areas in towns have traditionally been for pedestrians only as Spanish people love to take a formal *paseo* in the cool of the evening.

Today, you will find every kind of **hypermarket** *(un hipermercado)* or **supermarket** *(un supermercado)* and shops from all over Europe set up in designated retail park areas on the outskirts of town. These retail parks have cornered at least 32% of the retail market and are usually open from 10am to 10pm.

In every town, there will be a variety of **specialist shops**, such as the *estanco* – where you can buy stamps *(los sellos)*, as well as cigarettes *(los cigarillos)*. Another feature is the *quiosco*, which sells all kinds of newspapers and magazines *(los periódicos y las revistas)*, and no Spanish high street is without its *ONCE* lottery booth.

Banks *(el banco)* and **post offices** *(Correos)* have set opening hours – usually from 8am to 2pm. The *Correos* has a distinctive logo and yellow letterboxes.

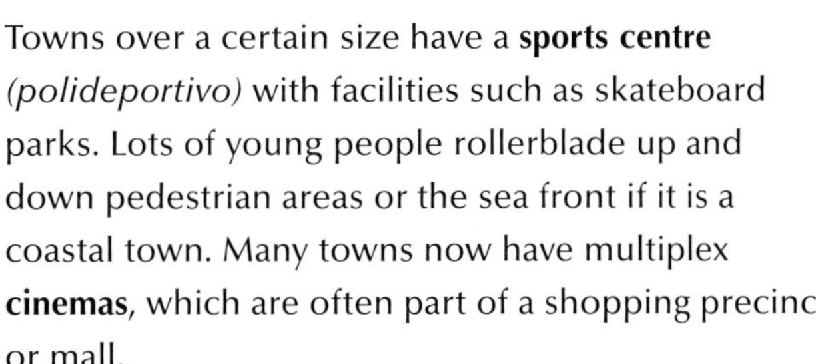

Towns over a certain size have a **sports centre** *(polideportivo)* with facilities such as skateboard parks. Lots of young people rollerblade up and down pedestrian areas or the sea front if it is a coastal town. Many towns now have multiplex **cinemas**, which are often part of a shopping precinct or mall.

Public libraries have recently been given a funding boost and most towns have one attached to the town hall or nearby.

Parks have always been a special feature in Spanish towns and they often have a lake or fountain. This is particularly evident in parks in southern Spain because the Moors delighted in water.

Read the information on pages 44 and 45 and complete the quiz.

1 What are the main features of a typical Spanish town? How does this compare with where you live?
2 Why do you think Spanish people like market day?
3 How often is rubbish collected in Spain? How does this compare to the UK?
4 Write down a list of shops near you and then look for the Spanish equivalent in a dictionary or on page 45.
5 Why are parks an important feature of Spanish towns?

Traditionally, people in towns have tended to live in flats, which accounts for a certain amount of the population density (see page 42). Apartment blocks can vary from ugly high-rise blocks to very luxurious and spacious homes in the centre of town.

Today, more and more small town houses are being built in the suburbs *(las afueras)*. There are new towns, such as Las Rosas or Pozuelo de Alarcón, outside Madrid, which have been specially built to house overspill. People who prefer to commute in to the city, or young couples who cannot afford the prices in town, favour these new towns.

Bilbao, in the north of Spain, is a large city and conurbation with a population of over 2 million, although it doesn't really feel like one because it stretches for about 14 km along the once polluted River Nervión. On both sides of the river are green hills rising up behind high-rise apartment blocks. Nearer the sea, the shipyards, docks and busy port are a few reminders of its industrial past. Bilbao has a remarkable modern museum – the Guggenheim.

Spain's leading architects

- Ricardo Bofill
- Santiago Calatrava
- Rafael Moneo
- Oriol Bohígas
- Alejandro de la Sota

Valencia (population 800 000) is Spain's third largest city. It rises out of the most fertile patch of land in Europe – *la huerta* – and is situated on the east coast by the Mediterranean. The old sea front has been developed into one of the most exciting building projects in Spain.

Seville (population 700 000) is the regional capital of Andalusia and was home to Expo '92, which helped to regenerate the city. There are many wonderful monuments and Seville boasts two of the largest festivals in Spain – the *Semana Santa* at Easter and the *Feria de abril*.

Montjuich in Barcelona

Barcelona

Barcelona is the fourth most densely populated city in the world. It has a central population of 1.9 million and a population of 4.8 million in the greater Barcelona area. It is the capital of Catalonia.

A thriving port and a prosperous commercial centre, Barcelona has a unique cultural sophistication and in many respects has always been a little ahead of the rest of Spain (although Madrid would dispute this claim).

There is a huge range of architectural styles to appreciate, from the Gothic quarter *(el barrio gótico)* and the Art Nouveau *(modernista)* of the elegant Eixample to the eccentric style of Gaudí epitomised by the Sagrada Familia. Today, there is also the unmistakable style of modern architecture, for example, in the Olympic Village. Many museums are devoted to some of the world's most famous artists, among them Picasso, Dalí, Miró and Tàpies.

Barcelona is a cosmopolitan city bubbling with energy and life – *Barcelona Més que Mai* (Barcelona more than ever) says one slogan. A walk up the famous Ramblas is the best way to begin to appreciate all this city has to offer.

The Casa Milá in Barcelona

► Las Ramblas in Barcelona

Read the information on pages 46 and 47 and complete the quiz.

1. What are the most common types of accommodation in Spanish cities?
2. What are *'las afueras'*?
3. Where is Seville? Which festivals are important there?
4. Write a short description of Barcelona.
5. Choose another Spanish city and use the Internet or library to find out more about it. Make up a slogan for it.
6. Use the Internet or library to find out more facts about Gaudí or one of the architects listed in the box on page 46.

12 Madrid

La Plaza Mayor

The patron saint of Madrid is San Isidro (see page 28).

La Puerta del Sol

Greater Madrid statistics

1561 population: 20 000

1960 population: 2 500 000

2001 population: 5 423 384

Central population: 2 938 723

13% of the population of Spain lives in Madrid.

Surface area: 605.8 km^2

Height above sea level: 655 metres

Weather: very cold winters and extremely hot summers

Madrid has everything – wealthy tree-lined avenues *(avenidas* or *paseos)*, huge glass skyscrapers *(rascacielos)*, elegant shops and fascinating markets, a wealth of museums *(museos)*, historic quarters *(barrios)* and many wonderful parks *(parques)*.

The symbol of Madrid is a bronze statue of a bear reaching for the fruit of a strawberry tree *(madroño)*. Located in the Puerta del Sol, it is at the very centre of Spain and is a popular meeting point for the people of Madrid *(los madrileños)*.

In the tenth century, Madrid *('Magerit'* in Arabic) was the site of a Moorish fortress. The city only began to prosper and flourish in 1561 when King Felipe II chose it as the capital because of its geographical location at the centre of the country. Today, Madrid is still the geographical, political, economical and cultural heart of Spain, where the rail and road networks meet. General Franco consolidated the importance of Madrid as the capital of the country.

Since Spain's transition to democracy, Madrid has become more than just the capital city, it is also one of the seventeen autonomous regions – the *Comunidad de Madrid*. The province is home to some magnificent scenery, mountains and parklands, as well as places of historical importance, such as the Escorial Palace and the Valley of the Fallen (see page 50).

The *madrileños* are a wonderful mix of people who have migrated to the city from all over Spain. Once a year, they celebrate the *Dos de mayo*, the name given to the Madrid uprising against Napoleon's occupation in 1808.

In 1992, Madrid was European Capital of Culture.

The **Prado Museum** holds a collection of masterpieces by Spain's great Golden Age artists, such as Goya, El Greco and Velazquez. It has a collection of over 7 000 paintings and is considered to be one of the world's richest art galleries. The historical power of Spain over the centuries is reflected in the large collection of 'foreign' art that it amassed over the years.

Parks and layout

Madrid has an abundance of parks and open spaces and prides itself on being one of Europe's greenest capitals. The **Casa de Campo**, a huge open park land, lies to the north-west of the city, the **Campo del Moro** is to the west of the centre and the **Parque del Retiro** is to the east. During the stifling, hot summer months, the Parque del Retiro is a bustling retreat for the city's occupants. *Madrileños* can walk through the park, hire a boat on the lake, listen to some busking, watch street performers or simply sit and have a cooling summer drink, such as *horchata*, in one of the many kiosks and bars.

▶ Parque del Retiro

The **Palacio Real** is a Bourbon palace, built in 1734. It replaced the fifteenth-century Gothic palace, which in turn was built on the original site of the Moorish *alcázar*.

The centre of Madrid can be divided into two sections – Old Madrid to the west, and Bourbon Madrid to the east. The River Manzanares skirts round the west to the south-east. There are many styles of architecture along the *Gran Vía* and the *Calle de Alcalá*, running from west to east, and the *Castellana*, running from north to south.

Art

Madrid has the greatest collection of art galleries anywhere in the world – the Prado, the Reina Sofía and the Museo de Thyssen-Bornemisza, which together form the 'golden triangle' of galleries.

Read the information on pages 48 and 49 and complete the quiz.

1 Read the following sentences and decide if they are true or false. Compare your ideas with a partner and correct any false information.
   - a The symbol of Madrid is a silver pear.
   - b 13% of the Spanish population live in the *Comunidad de Madrid*.
   - c Madrid was the site of a Roman fortress in the eleventh century.
   - d Madrid became capital in 1951.
   - e In 1992, Madrid was European Capital of Culture.
   - f *El Dos de mayo* rose up against the British.

2 Why did King Felipe II choose Madrid to be the capital of Spain? Do you think this was a good idea? Where is the capital city of your country located?

3 Name three things you can do in the Parque del Retiro.

4 What is the 'golden triangle'?

People watching

A great Spanish pastime is people watching and there is no better place to do this than at **el Rastro**, the spectacular Sunday street market, or the **Plaza Mayor** in the city centre.

Madrid has more bars per head of population than any other city in the world – about 4000 in total. The most popular ones with *Madrileños* have *terrazas* – the area outside a bar, with tables and chairs.

Getting around

The underground system in Madrid has eleven lines and 120 stations, and is probably one of the best in the world (see page 55). Trains start running at 6.30am and stop running at 1.30am. You can buy single tickets *(sencillo)* or monthly passes *(bono mensual)*. It is also possible to buy a carnet of ten tickets for travel on both trains and buses.

The **Estación de Atocha** was Madrid's first railway station, first used in 1851. The old station underwent extensive modernisation in the 1980s and includes an impressive 600 m^2 indoor tropical garden.

El Escorial

Around Madrid

Madrid is more than just a capital city. There are many treasures outside the city centre.

El Escorial

This huge, impressive palace and monastery was built between 1563 and 1584 for King Felipe II. The palace has 16 courtyards, 2673 windows, 1200 doors and 86 staircases.

Close by is the **Valle de los Caídos** (the Valley of the Fallen), the war monument built by Franco to honour the dead of the Civil War.

There are two summer palaces – **El Pardo** to the north-west, and **Aranjuez**, set in beautiful parkland to the south.

◄ Aranjuez summer palace

Plaza Mayor, Chinchón

Alcázar, Toledo

Further afield

The sixteenth-century **Alcalá de Henares** is a beautiful university town that was home to some of Spain's greatest writers. Lope de Vega (1562–1635) studied at the university and Miguel de Cervantes (1547–1616) was born there.

Chinchón has a unique porticoed Plaza Mayor.

Toledo is considered one of the most beautiful and historically important towns in Spain. Between the twelfth and fifteenth centuries, it was home to Moors, Christians and Jews. Their legacy is seen in the winding streets, the cathedral, the old fortress *(alcázar)*, El Greco's house and, of course, the spectacular hillside views of the surrounding countryside.

Segovia has also had both Moorish and Christian influences over the centuries. Its crowning glory is the Roman aqueduct, with 165 arches and stretching 813 metres in length and 128 metres high. Segovia is renowned for its cuisine, especially lamb and suckling pig.

► Roman aqueduct, Segovia

Read the information on pages 50 and 51 and complete the quiz.

1 What is special about Madrid's *Estación de Atocha?*

2 Using the information on pages 50 and 51, find out what the following numbers represent:

120 16 86 1851 1200 813 2673

3 Write a short paragraph, in English, explaining which tourist attraction on page 50 or 51 you would most like to visit and why.

4 Use the Internet or library to find out more about the life of either Lope de Vega or Miguel de Cervantes. Write a short paragraph using the information.

13 Travel and transport

Driving

In the last twenty years, Spain has transformed its road, rail and transport systems. The government realised how important this would be in the run up to international events such as the World Cup (1982), the Olympics (1992) and the Seville Expo (1992).

Between 1980 and 1990, the number of cars doubled, but still only 65% of households had a car. In 2001, there was an estimated 13 696 414 male drivers and 7 852 025 female drivers. People drive on the right-hand side of the road in Spain.

In Spain, it has long been necessary to pass both a practical and also a written exam in order to get a driving licence. The severity of the test, however, has not had a great effect on what actually happens on the roads. Unfortunately, Spain has one of the worst accident rates in Europe, rivalled only by Portugal.

The road network covers 300 000 km, of which 6 000 km are motorways *(autopistas)*. These motorways are mostly toll roads *(peaje)*, built by private companies. This privatisation has made them among the best in Europe. The downside is that they are expensive and this consequently causes other major roads *(autovías)* to be very busy. To make life even quicker, there is a *telepeaje* system that reads the number plate of a car and sends the bill later.

Spain and France have just opened a new tunnel through the Pyrenees, linking the two countries (see page 54).

Drink driving continues to be a problem and Spanish law is quite strict. There is an instant fine of 600€ for people who are caught over the limit. The legal limit is about two beers.

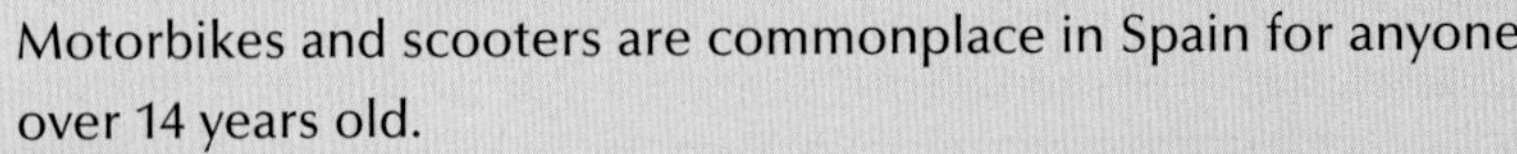

Motorbikes and scooters are commonplace in Spain for anyone over 14 years old.

Ferries and ships

Spain has several major ports, of which Algeciras, Barcelona, Cadiz and Bilbao are the largest. Domestic and international ferry services link the mainland to the Balearic and Canary Islands, North Africa, the UK and South America. The two routes that link the UK with Spain are Plymouth to Santander, and Portsmouth to Bilbao. The crossings take about 24 hours but are an easy and relaxing way to get a family and car to Spain.

The crossing to the Balearic Islands takes up to ten hours but the ferries have bars, cabins, cinemas, swimming pools and other facilities to make the lengthy crossing as pleasurable as possible.

Malaga is Spain's main cruise liner port and serves the whole of the Mediterranean and the Atlantic.

The airlines

Owing to Spain's size and mountainous terrain, air travel is a convenient and easy form of transport. There are over forty airports in Spain. The Spanish international airline is Iberia and it has one of the best safety records in the world. Traditionally, Iberia had a monopoly on all internal travel, however, new airlines, such as Spanair and Air Europa, have increased domestic competition.

Recently, as in the UK, budget airlines have forced Iberia to reduce its fares. Airlines such as easyJet, Spanair and now Virgin have made the Spanish air travel market very competitive, which is good news for tourists! Spain naturally has good connections with North, Central and South America but has more limited connections with the rest of the world.

The principal airport on mainland Spain for international flights is Barajas airport in Madrid. However, Palma de Mallorca handles the largest number of people – well over 15 million a year.

Read the information on pages 52 and 53 and complete the quiz.

1 a Explain why the Spanish transport infrastructure has been greatly modernised in the last 20 years.
   b What is the difference between an *autopista* and an *autovía*?

2 Write a paragraph on one of the following points:
   a What are the pros and cons of making motorists pay to use motorways? Do you think it is a system that should be used in the UK?
   b How do you think the Spanish government could reduce the number of deaths on the roads?

3 What is the busiest airport in Spain? How many people use it each year?

Trains

The rail network was underfunded during the Franco era and it was slow and well below European standards. However, during the last ten years, journey times have been reduced by 50%.

An AVE train

The TALGO (the intercity service) and the AVE (high-speed, luxury trains) are responsible for this reduction in journey times. In 1992, the *Tren de Alta Velocidad Espanola (AVE)* was introduced on the journey between Madrid and Seville – a showpiece for Expo '92. The journey time is only two hours and twenty-five minutes. The train can travel up to 350 km/h and if it is more than five minutes late, full refunds are given. This type of train is set to be in use between Madrid and Barcelona in 2004, and between Malaga and Valencia by 2005.

Other long-distance trains *(trenes de largo recorrido)* are slower and stop at lots of stations but are considerably cheaper.

The Spanish State railways *(Red Nacional de Ferrocarriles Espanoles* or *RENFE)* have over 24 000 km of track and 2 500 stations. The network includes all major cities. The regions of Valencia, the Basque region and Catalonia also have their own separate regional companies. In 1999, the Spanish railways had the best safety record in Europe.

Tickets are bought at *la taquilla*.

Ask for *una ida sola* or *una ida y vuelta*.

There are also two special trains, for enjoyment more than practicality. The *Al Andalus Express* provides a luxury tour of Andalusia and stops at Granada, Seville, Cordoba and Jerez. The journey is breathtaking and can last four to five days. The *Transcantábrico* travels along the north coast of Spain from San Sebastian to Santiago de Compostela.

The most recent and perhaps most controversial rail development is the new eight-kilometre, £170 million Somport tunnel which runs through the Pyrenees. It opened in January 2003 following fifteen years of development, planning and environmental protest. It is due to carry up to 2 500 vehicles a day. Naturally, conservationists are concerned about the effect that this will have on the surrounding environment.

► A protest against the Somport tunnel

Urban transport

Generally, public transport in big cities is excellent. Most have efficient bus and rail services, some have underground systems *(metros)* and some even have trams *(tranvías)*. Urban transport in Madrid, Barcelona and other cities is inexpensive, efficient and rates among the best in the world.

Metro

The Barcelona and Valencia metro systems are relatively modern compared to the Madrid metro system (see page 50). On all of the systems, there are a variety of ticket types for single journeys and multiple journeys of one stop or more. All the lines are integrated and the same ticket can be used on all services.

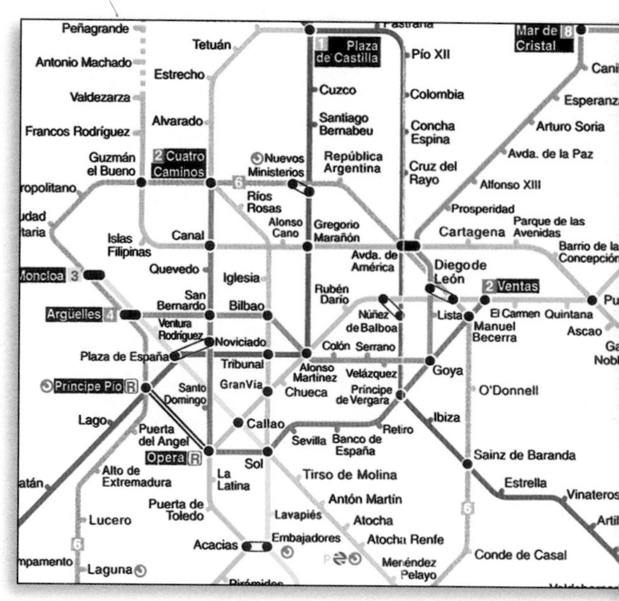

Buses

The buses in all major cities are excellent and all towns have long-distance coach services *(autocar)* that are fast and frequent.

Like the metro tickets, bus tickets are the same price, however long the journey. Be careful – unlike in the UK, passengers get on and off at both the front and rear doors.

Trams

Some cities still have a functioning tram system. Air-conditioned trams were reintroduced in Valencia in 1994 after a 20-year break, and there is also a tram system in Barcelona.

Taxis

Taxi stops *(paradas de taxis)* are found outside airports and stations. Spanish taxis are relatively inexpensive and it is not usual to tip. In Madrid, there are approximately 15 000 licensed cars.

Driving

Owing to the custom of long lunch breaks with many people eating at home, it is said that Spain has four rush hours:

8.30–9.30am; 12.30–2.30pm; 3.30–4pm; and 6.30–8pm.

In cities, traffic jams *(embotellamientos)* are frequent; the infrastructure and the small narrow, cobbled streets were not designed for the increasingly large number of vehicles. Parking is also a major headache in cities, although more and more large underground car parks are being built.

As in all large cities, urban pollution is a growing concern. Madrid has a special uniformed force whose job it is to spot-check fuel emissions on cars.

Read the information on pages 54 and 55 and complete the quiz.

1 Using a Spanish dictionary, translate the different methods of transport mentioned on pages 52 to 55.
2 Using the Internet or library, find out some more information about either the *Al Andalus Express* or the *Transcantábrico* trains (times, prices, stops, different activities on board, etc.).
3 Write a paragraph on the problem of urban traffic and possible solutions.

14 History

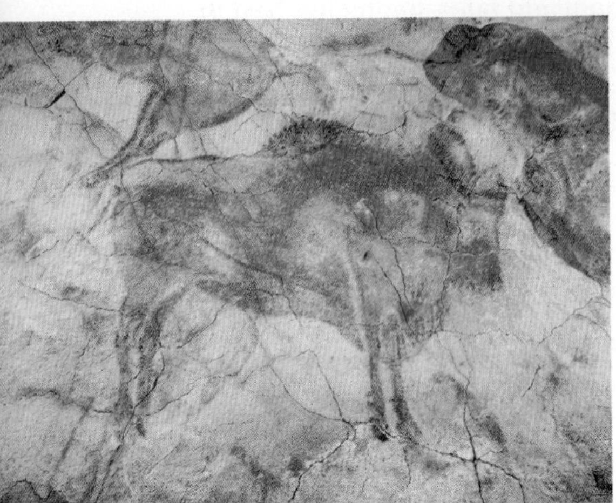

Altamira cave painting

Spain was first inhabited by hunter-gatherers in around 800 000BC. Skeletons and cave paintings are still found in parts of Spain. Since then, it has been characterised by foreign influences, which is one of the reasons why Spain is such a rich, culturally diverse country.

Romans

The Romans remained in Spain for five centuries, from around 218BC to 476AD. During this time, they developed cities and laid the foundation for the Spanish language and culture.

Moors

Arabs and Berber tribes (known as the Moors) crossed from North Africa in 711. They stayed in Spain for nearly eight centuries. The Moors were brilliant scientists, mathematicians, architects and artists and during this time they created the most advanced civilisations in medieval Europe. They introduced medicine to the western world as well as the water wheel, which revolutionised agriculture.

In 1492, Christopher Columbus, an Italian explorer, discovered the Americas, bringing great wealth to Spain. This began the period known as the Golden Age.

Christians

From the eleventh century, the Christian kingdoms of the north gradually won back their land until finally, in 1492, the army of King Fernando and Queen Isabel *(Los Reyes Católicos)* defeated the Moors in Granada. This period of 300 years is known as the Reconquest.

The year 1492 is a most important date in Spanish history. With the Moors driven out, the country was gradually unified. It also marks the discovery of the New World by Christopher Columbus. This brought great wealth to Spain, which was slowly drained away by constant warfare in Europe.

The Golden Age

The seventeenth century was a period dominated by economic problems and war but also by artistic and literary brilliance.

Decline and troubled times (1700 to 1936)

The War of Spanish Succession ended with victory for the Bourbons and the loss of Gibraltar. The empire of Central and South America retained close links with Spain but gradually sought independence. Through wars and disputes over succession, Spain's once massive empire crumbled.

The Inquisition was a religious police force that made sure everyone converted to and observed the Catholic faith. This involved brutal torturing, burning at the stake and expulsion of any Moors and Jews who didn't want to convert to Christianity.

Early Spanish leaders

Trajan (53–117)

The first Hispanic Roman Emperor improved public administration and extended the empire.

El Cid (1043–1099)

This nobleman, soldier and mercenary was renowned for his courage and bravery. He changed sides after a feud with King Fernando and fought for the Moors. He then returned to help the Christians take control of Valencia in 1094.

Alfonso X (1221–1284)

Known as Alfonso the Wise or Learned *(Alfonso el Sabio)*, Alfonso X transformed the areas of economy and law and made great contributions to the cultural development of Spain.

Isabel and Fernando

The marriage in 1469 of the royal cousins, Fernando of Aragon (1452–1516) and Isabel of Castile (1451–1504) helped to unite Spain. Spain became one of the best-administered countries in Europe during their reign.

Carlos V (1516–1556)

Carlos V (also known as the Holy Roman Emperor Charles I) was leader of the world's most diverse empire since Roman times.

Felipe II (1556–1598)

As the husband of Mary Tudor (Mary I) of England, King Felipe II (left) sought to extend an already vast Catholic empire. When he inherited the throne of Portugal, the Iberian Peninsula had one ruler for the next sixty years. However, his attempt to invade Protestant England ended in the defeat of the Armada in 1588.

Read the information on pages 56 and 57 and complete the quiz.

1 Complete the sentences with names/races from the text.

Isabel and Fernando	Felipe II	The Romans
Columbus	The Moors	Trajan
Alfonso X	El Cid	Carlos V

a Stayed in Spain for five centuries.

b Were brilliant scientists, inventors and architects.

c Reunited Spain after defeating the Moors in 1492.

d Discovered the Americas.

e Was King of Spain when the Armada fought and lost a battle against England.

f Was also known as the Holy Roman Emperor.

g Was known for his achievements in culture, law and economics.

h Fought for both the Moors and the Christians.

i Became the first Hispanic Roman Emperor.

2 Write a paragraph, in English, on the following topic: Who do you think was the greatest Spanish leader or historical figure and why? Write about what they achieved and also what they failed to achieve.

The Civil War (1936–1939)

In 1936, the Nationalists rose up against the Republican government. The Nationalist forces received support from both Nazi Germany and Fascist Italy. Britain, France and America pursued a policy of non-intervention and refused to help, fearing that their support might lead to a European war. Russia helped the Republican forces by providing them with military hardware, advisers and logistics experts, in return for gold. The United States provided more than 2 000 volunteers and France provided some aircraft and artillery.

In 1937, at the request of Franco, the Nazi Condor legion bombed the small town of Guernica, in the Basque region, to help the advancing Nationalists. The bombing on 26 April marked the first ever saturation bombing of a civilian population and was immortalised by Picasso's painting (below left).

Towards the end of the war, the Republican army was involved in its own internal power struggle and was never able to mount any sustained counteroffensive. Barcelona fell to the Nationalists in January 1939, and Valencia, the temporary capital, fell in March. Madrid remained the strong hold of the Republicans until the government surrendered on the last day of March 1939.

After the war, many Republicans were executed. It is estimated that 600 000 people died in combat, bombings, and executions, tens of thousands died of starvation, and several hundred thousand more fled from Spain.

In the 1950s, the USA, wanting to establish more military bases in Europe, finally decided to give Spain much-needed aid and gradually the economy began to recover.

General Franco

General Franco

Francisco Franco had a reputation as a highly professional, career-oriented combat soldier and first-rate officer. At the age of 33, he became the youngest general in Europe since Napoleon Bonaparte. In October 1936, Franco was named Head of State by the Nationalist forces, with the rank of *Generalissimo* and the title *el Caudillo* (the leader).

Following the Republican defeat in 1939, General Franco became the dictator of Spain until his death in 1975. Under Franco, no other political parties were permitted. For much of his dictatorship, Spain was isolated economically, culturally and politically, which kept Spain out of the Second World War.

King Juan Carlos I

Post-Franco Spain

In July 1969, Franco named Prince Juan Carlos de Bourbon as his successor: a legitimate heir to the throne. On 22 November 1975, following the death of Franco, the Prince took the oath as King of Spain. There was nothing to indicate that he would be the architect of such a dramatic transformation of Spain, given that the young King had been hand-picked, schooled and educated by Franco. Finally, Spain had a constitutional monarchy and could begin the transition to democracy.

Adolfo Suárez González, who had previously served under Franco, became Prime Minister and the combination of his political expertise and Juan Carlos's determination and ability to maintain the loyalty of the army made a peaceful transition to democracy possible. Previously-banned political parties were reinstated and power was devolved to the regional autonomies.

In 1982, the Socialist Workers' Party won the general election and Felipe González came to power. During his time as Prime Minister, Spain joined the world stage. In 1982, Spain joined NATO and also hosted the World Cup, and in 1986 it became a member of the European Union. In 1992, Barcelona hosted the Olympic Games, Seville was home to World Expo and Madrid was European Capital of Culture. In 1996, the Conservative José María Aznar was elected Prime Minister.

23 February 1981 – *El Tejerazo* (the night of the Tricorns)

In 1981, there was a failed attempt to overthrow the government. Colonel Tejero held parliament at gunpoint for several hours, but King Juan Carlos did not support the rebels and the coup failed.

The Sepharad '92

One almost forgotten but most significant event took place in 1992. Spain welcomed back the Jews and the King apologised for the injustice done to them when they were expelled 500 years previously.

Read the information on pages 58 and 59 and complete the quiz.

1 **a** When was the Spanish Civil War?

b Which countries helped each of the sides during the conflict?

c Why is Guernica (the place and the painting) significant?

2 Why was the naming of Juan Carlos as heir to Franco a turning point in Spanish modern history?

3 What has happened to Spain since the early 1980s?

4 Correct the mistakes in the following sentences:

a Germany helped Spain in the Second World War.

b In 1992, Spain joined NATO and hosted the World Cup.

c The Conservative government stayed in power for 14 years (1982–1996).

d Russia sent weapons to Franco's army during the war.

e In the 1950s, Spain received much-needed aid from the UK.

f Madrid remained the strong hold of the Republicans until the government surrendered on the first day of May, 1939.

15 How Spain is governed today

A year after the death of Franco in November 1975, political parties were legalised in Spain and their first task was to create a new constitution for the country. The new constitution of 31 October 1978 transformed Spain from a dictatorship to a democratic government. Today, it has one of the most liberal constitutions in Western Europe.

Spain's three police forces

Local police *(guardia urbana* or *policía municipal)* - attached to towns with over 5 000 residents and wear a blue uniform

National police *(policía nacional)* - attached to towns with over 20 000 residents and wear a blue uniform

Civil Guard *(Guardia Civil)* - patrol highways and rural areas and wear an olive green uniform

Some autonomies have their own special forces.

The government

The central government has overall responsibility for running the country (foreign affairs, external trade, defence, justice, law, shipping and aviation) but Spain has created a unique system of home rule for the regions (see page 61).

At present, Spain has a fairly healthy Left/Right divide, which keeps a check on the balance of power. After the general elections in March 1996, the Conservative *Partido Popular (PP)*, led by José María Aznar, won a narrow victory over the Socialists *(Partido Socialista Obrero Español* or *PSOE)*, who had governed Spain since 1982. However, after the elections in March 2000 the *Partido Popular* gained an overall majority.

The United Left *(Izquierda Unida)* is the third largest national party and there are also important regional parties representing Catalonia and the Basque Country.

Spain's Royal Family

King Juan Carlos I is married to Princess Sofía of Greece, a cousin of the Duke of Edinburgh. They live just outside Madrid in the *Palacio de la Zarzuela* and leave the large *Palacio Real* for formal occasions only. Their three children are Elena, the eldest, who is married to a banker; Cristina, the second daughter, who is married to a popular handball player and is a civil servant and finally, Felipe, the Crown Prince *(el Principe de Asturias)*, who is the heir to the throne and will be married in June 2004. In Spain, women cannot succeed to the throne.

Crown Prince Felipe and Letizia Ortiz announce their engagement.

Spain has been a member of the United Nations since 1955, of NATO since 1982 and of the European Union since 1986. Spain is also a permanent observer of the Organisation of American States (OAS), a body which looks after the interests of all countries in North, Central and South America.

Comunidades Autónomas

One of the most important tasks of the newly-founded democracy was to give power to the regions. Today, Spain is divided into seventeen autonomous regions called *Comunidades Autónomas (CCAA)*, which have not only been defined by the geographical areas but also by history. In fact, they more or less correspond to the old kingdoms that developed during the Middle Ages at the time of the Reconquest.

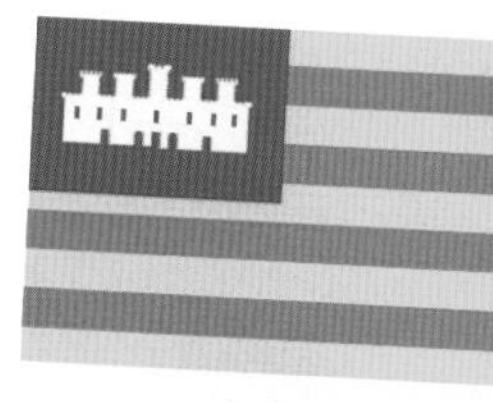

Each *Comunidad Autónoma* has its own government *(gobierno* or *junta)* with between 33 and 135 seats, depending on the size of the region, and its own parliament. The *CCAA* hold an election every four years. They elect a president and control their own administration and supreme court to varying degrees. For example, the major autonomous regions of the Basque Country, Catalonia, Galicia and Andalusia control some of their own taxes and have the right to use their own language in education and administration. Each of the *CCAA* has their own flag (see below) and capital city. The regions are funded by the central government, however, some get more money than others and this can cause problems as the poorer and more sparsely populated regions are worse off.

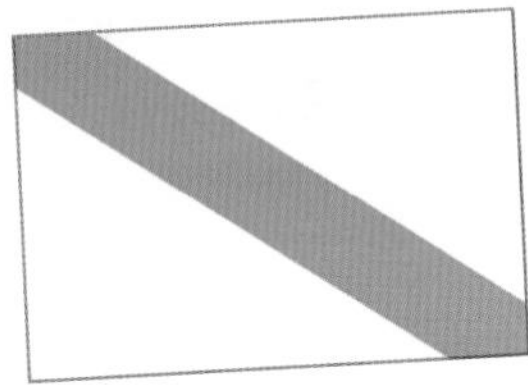

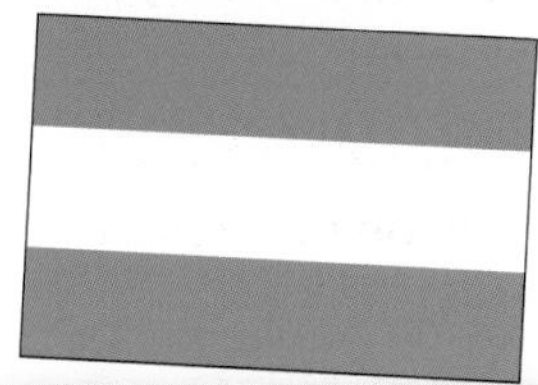

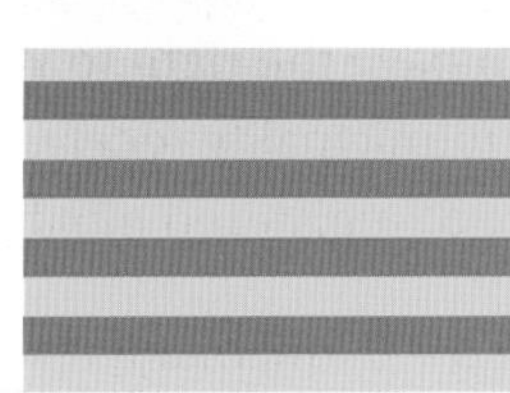

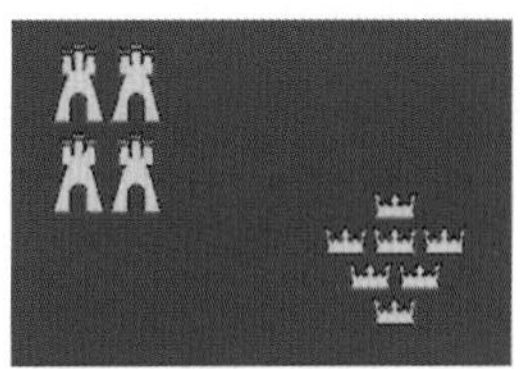

Read the information on pages 60 and 61 and complete the quiz.

1. Why do you think it is important to have a constitution? Does the UK have one?
2. How many types of police force are there in Spain? What do they each do?
3. Research a bit more about the Spanish Royal Family. How does it compare with Britain's Royal Family?
4. Debate the pros and cons of having a royal family.
5. How many regional autonomies are there? Do you think they are a good idea?

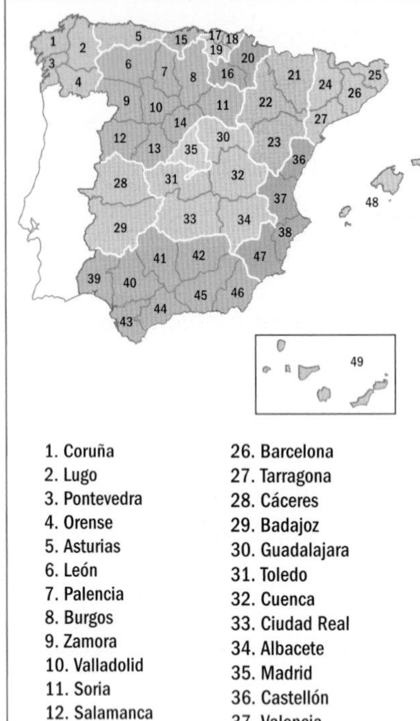

1. Coruña
2. Lugo
3. Pontevedra
4. Orense
5. Asturias
6. León
7. Palencia
8. Burgos
9. Zamora
10. Valladolid
11. Soria
12. Salamanca
13. Àvila
14. Segovia
15. Cantabria
16. La Rioja
17. Vizcaya
18. Guipúzcoa
19. Alava
20. Navarra
21. Huesca
22. Zaragossa
23. Teruel
24. Lérida (Lleida)
25. Gerona (Girona)
26. Barcelona
27. Tarragona
28. Cáceres
29. Badajoz
30. Guadalajara
31. Toledo
32. Cuenca
33. Ciudad Real
34. Albacete
35. Madrid
36. Castellón
37. Valencia
38. Alicante
39. Huelva
40. Seville
41. Córdoba
42. Jaén
43. Cadiz
44. Málaga
45. Granada
46. Almería
47. Murcia
48. Baleares
49. Canarias

The *CCAA* are subdivided into 49 provinces *(provincias)*, most of which are named after their capital city (see left). Each province has its own administration which is responsible for a range of services, such as health (hospitals, nursing homes and homes for the elderly), public works such as roads, sports facilities such as public swimming pools, and social clubs for young people.

There are also 8 000 municipalities with elected councillors *(concejales)* and each one has a mayor *(alcalde)* whose offices are in the town hall *(ayuntamiento)*.

▶ The town hall in Moguer

Everyone who is on the official register *(padrón municipal)* is also then included on the electoral roll *(censo electoral)* and has the right to vote if they are over 18. Foreigners who are local residents are encouraged to register and they then have the right to vote in local elections. The amount of money each municipality receives from central government depends on the number of registered inhabitants.

Municipalities with over 5 000 inhabitants must provide public parks, a public library and a market. Those with over 20 000 inhabitants also need to provide civil protection, social services, fire prevention services and sports facilities, plus a public slaughter house!

There are 60 constituencies that are now represented in the European Parliament. EU residents of Spain are allowed to vote in European elections for Members of the European Parliament (MEPs) but cannot vote in Spanish general elections.

Did you know?

The death penalty is forbidden in Spain.

Compulsory military service *(la mili)* was abolished in 2001.

Everybody over 14 years old must have an identity card *(carné de identidad)*.

Parliament

After a general election, the results are officially made public five days later to allow time for recounts and any disputed results. Once the new members have been sworn in, the King of Spain meets with the party leaders and asks one of them, usually the leader of the largest party, to form a government. This is then ratified by Parliament. The leader of the party of government becomes the Spanish Prime Minister *(el presidente del gobierno)* and lives in the official residence of the Moncloa Palace in Madrid.

The **Constitutional Court** *(el tribunal constitucional)* is responsible for making sure that any laws passed by Parliament comply with the constitution and any international agreements that Spain may have agreed to. Spain also has a **Judiciary** *(Consejo general del Poder Judicial)* with twenty members, which is headed by the president of the **Supreme Court** *(tribunal supreme)* and is totally independent of the government.

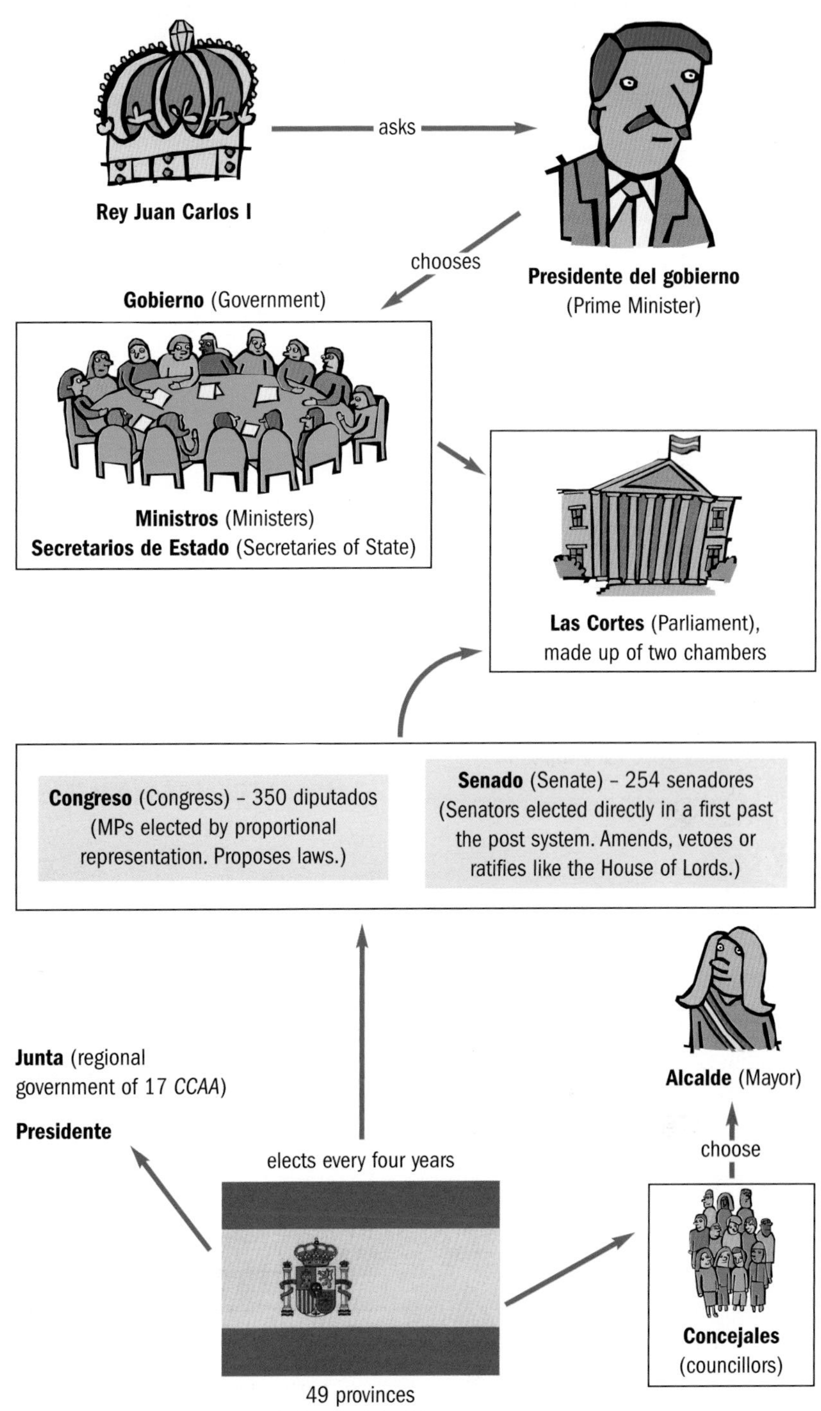

Read the information on pages 62 and 63 and complete the quiz.

1. Do we have compulsory military service in the UK? Do you think military service is a good idea?
2. Debate the pros and cons of carrying ID cards.
3. Does Spain allow the death penalty? When was it abolished in the UK?
4. If you lived in Spain, which elections would you be allowed to vote in if you were over 18?
5. Compare the systems of government in Spain and the UK. What are the differences and similarities?

16 The media and the arts

You don't need a television licence in Spain.

Football probably draws the biggest audiences – live matches are broadcast up to six evenings a week. The Spanish also love soap operas *(culebrones)* such as *'El super'* and *'Famosas y familia'*, which receive regular viewing figures of 20 million (*EastEnders* gets 12.7 million).

During the forty years of General Franco's dictatorship, newspapers and the media were heavily censored. Since freedom of the press was permitted in 1978, all aspects of Spanish media (television, radio and the press) have been playing catch-up with many other European countries.

Television

Television *(la televisión)* began as a regular service in 1956, and was heavily censored with very limited programme choice. A second channel started in 1965. Since the late 1970s, when censorship was lifted, Spanish television has been transformed. Nowadays, there is little censorship and it is not uncommon to see risqué game shows that wouldn't be acceptable in the UK. There are five national television channels. Spain has the fourth biggest number of television viewers in Europe (after Portugal, the UK and Italy).

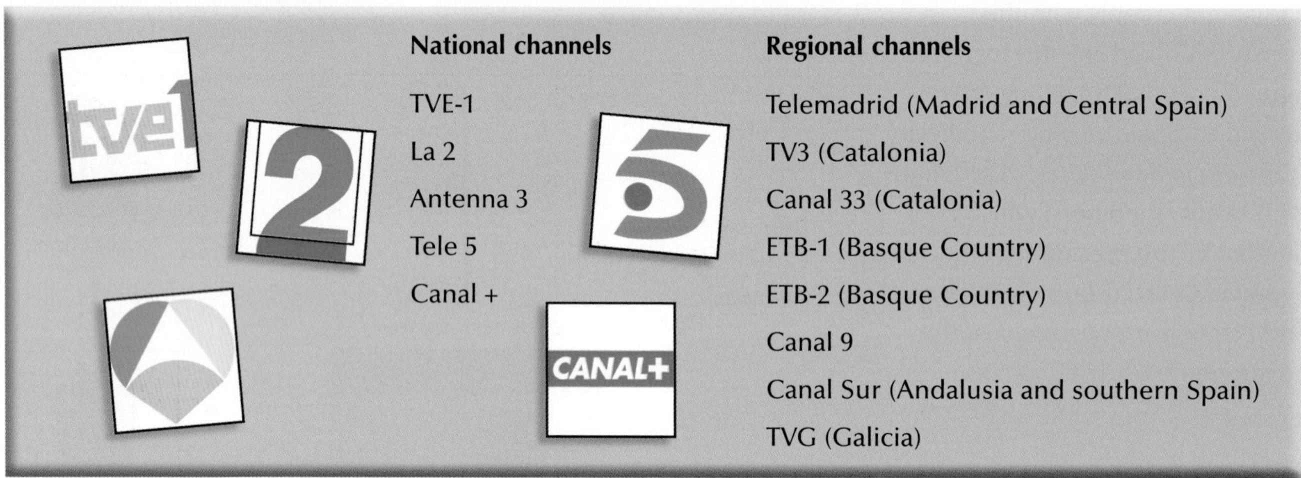

National channels

TVE-1
La 2
Antenna 3
Tele 5
Canal +

Regional channels

Telemadrid (Madrid and Central Spain)
TV3 (Catalonia)
Canal 33 (Catalonia)
ETB-1 (Basque Country)
ETB-2 (Basque Country)
Canal 9
Canal Sur (Andalusia and southern Spain)
TVG (Galicia)

Radio

The first radio station began in Barcelona in 1928 but the development of radio as a mass media tool was disrupted during the Civil War, and was heavily monitored under the Franco regime. The Spanish are a nation of radio listeners and there are over 1500 State-owned and private radio stations.

Well over half of the adult population listens to the radio every day – the highest number in Europe. More people listen to the radio than watch television and there are estimated to be around 35 million radios in Spain (for a population of 40 million).

Newspapers and magazines

El País, established in 1976, is the most widely sold newspaper, offering serious political analysis and international news. As there is only limited parliamentary control over the media, journalists have a very important role to play in commenting on and criticising government. Specialist daily newspapers dedicated to sport are very popular – particularly *AS* and *Marca*. The readership figures vary greatly from week to week, largely depending on the front cover. There are no tabloid newspapers like the *Sun* in Spain. The job of gossiping is left to the magazines.

Most of Spain's newspapers and magazines are sold through kiosks (*estancos* or *quioscos* – stands on street corners). The large number of British people in Spain makes it possible to buy most British newspapers, but they cost about three times more than in the UK.

Magazines are very popular. Most people opt for the television guides and weekly gossips *(prensa del corazón)*, such as '*¡Hola!*', '*Diez Minutos*' and '*Semana*'. They are similar to British magazines such as *Hello!* and *OK*, and sell over 2.5 million copies each week.

¡Hola! magazine was a Spanish creation which was started in 1944 by the Sánchez Junco family. A possible reason for its early success was that it allowed ordinary people some escapism from the monotony and troubles of their daily lives in Franco's Spain. In 1988, an English version *(Hello!)* was launched. Today, the shelves in both Spain and the UK are littered with gossip magazines, all following the same glossy format and allowing ordinary people a glance at the lives of the rich and famous.

Read the information on pages 64 and 65 and complete the quiz.

1 a How many national television channels are there in Spain?
  b What effect did censorship have on the development of the media?
  c Which form of media is the most popular in Spain?
  d What information can you remember about the gossip magazine *¡Hola!*?

2 Using a dictionary, make a list, in Spanish, of the different types of television programmes you watch during the week. Compare your list with a partner. Do you enjoy watching similar programmes?

3 Use the Internet to find out more about Spanish newspapers and magazines. Look for some websites of Spanish newspapers, such as *El País*.

4 Write a paragraph in English about why more people in Spain prefer listening to the radio than reading newspapers. Use the information on pages 64 and 65 and your own ideas.

5 Write a paragraph on the following topic:
Do you agree or disagree with censorship in the media?

Art

Spain has produced some of the world's greatest artists and their work can be seen in museums all over the world. Much of Spain's social and political history can be learnt by studying the art of the time.

El Greco (1541–1614)

El Greco was born in Greece but lived mostly in Toledo. His work shows the influence of religion on Spanish history.

Diego Velazquez (1599–1660)

Velazquez was the court painter to Felipe IV. *Las Meninas* is considered to be technically the best painting in the world.

Francisco de Goya (1746–1828)

Goya lived through a very violent period of Spanish history.

Pablo Picasso (1881–1973)

Picasso is considered to be the father of twentieth-century modern art. Many of his works are displayed in the Picasso Museum in Barcelona, the Centro de Arte Reina Sofía in Madrid and the new Picasso Museum in Malaga. In the Reina Sofía it is possible to see his greatest work – *Guernica* (see page 58).

Joan Miró (1893–1983)

Miró loved bright colours and shapes.

Salvador Dalí (1904–1989)

The bright, vivid colours and distorted images of Dalí's work are wonderful examples of Surrealism.

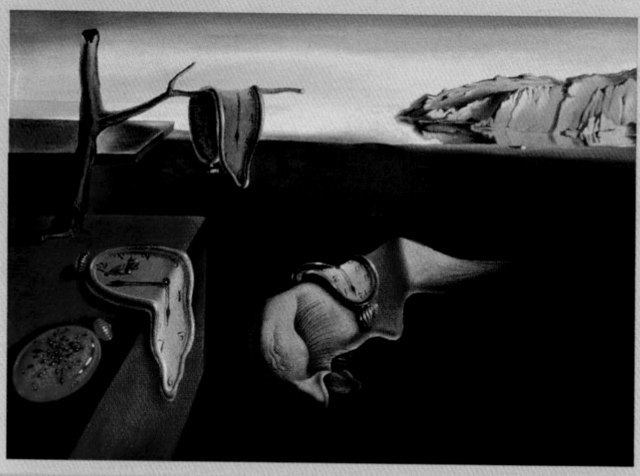

Sculpture

Two of the most well-known Spanish sculptors are **Eduardo Chillida** (1924–2002) and **Juan Muñoz** (1953–2001).

Cinema

During the Franco regime, the cinema was used as a means of mass propaganda and films were heavily censored. Nowadays, the Spanish are a nation of cinema lovers and Spain has developed a strong reputation in film production. Although Spain now boasts an extensive list of respected film directors, actors and producers, perhaps two figures stand out as being key to the development of Spanish cinema.

Luis Buñuel (1900–1983)
Buñuel was a master of twentieth-century cinema. Much of his work was produced abroad as there were great restrictions on film-making in Spain. Some of his best films are *Belle De Jour* (1967) and *That Obscure Object of Desire* (1977).

Pedro Almodóvar (1951–present)
In recent years, Spanish cinema has been transformed by the work of director Pedro Almodóvar. He was fortunate to be making films in post-1975 Spain when new literary and artistic freedoms were being exercised. His films are colourful, energetic and quirky, a style completely opposed to previous Spanish directors. This has helped make his films extremely popular outside Spain. His best-known films are *Hable con ella* (*Talk to her*, 2002), *Todo sobre mi madre* (*All about my mother*, 1999), *Mujeres al borde de un ataque de nervios* (*Women on the verge of a nervous breakdown*, 1988) and *Tacones lejanos* (*High heels*, 1991). Almodóvar is also responsible for turning actors such as Antonio Banderas and Penélope Cruz into international film stars.

Pedro Almodóvar

Read the information on pages 66 and 67 and complete the quiz.

1. **a** Why is Picasso an important Spanish figure?
   b What art movement did Dalí belong to?
2. Find out some more information about one of the artists or sculptors on page 66.
3. Why were Almodóvar's films well received outside Spain?
4. Using the information on pages 66 and 67 write five general knowledge questions to ask a partner. For example, where did El Greco live most of his life? When you have finished, swap questions with another pair and see if you can answer their questions.
5. Use the Internet or library to research other film directors such as Carlos Saura and Bigas Luna, or actors such as Fernando Rey, Javier Bardem and Carmen Maura.

17 Working in Spain

The Workers' Statute

Working conditions in Spain mostly depend on the 1980 Workers' Statute *(Estatuto de Trabajadores)*. Young people under the age of 16 cannot be employed, although many do help out in family businesses. Between 16 and 18 years old, young people need their parent's written permission to be able to work, although many ignore this. Those under the age of 18 are not officially allowed to work overtime, do night work or certain dangerous or unhealthy jobs.

The standard working week in Spain is 40 hours and the average with overtime is 43 hours. The normal working day is from 9.30am to around 1.30pm, and from 5.30pm until around 8pm.

Sometimes, in the hot summer months from June to September, people may work from 7am to 3pm (this is known as *horario intensivo*). However, this is all changing, in cities especially, as people move to a more internationally accepted continuous working day.

Overtime is not compulsory in Spain and it cannot exceed 80 hours a year. Workers are entitled to a minimum of one and a half days off each week, plus public holidays. Twelve hours must elapse between shifts. A full-time employee is entitled to 20 working days of paid annual holiday. Some businesses close down completely during August.

Annual holidays in Spain

- 20 paid working days
- 14 national and public holidays (7 national, 5 widely celebrated and 2 local)

When both annual and public holidays are taken into account, Spain has the most holidays of any country in the EU.

Spain has a statutory minimum wage *(salario mínimo)*, which is currently 500€ a month for an unskilled worker aged between 16 and 59. Most employees receive a month's extra salary *(paga extraordinaria)* twice a year, at Christmas and before the August summer holiday.

The disabled *(los discapacitados)* make up about 9% of the population, of whom around 30 000 are in protected employment *(empleo protegido)*.

Una huelga – a strike

Unemployment

Spain's recent economic recovery has helped to bring down the unemployment figure from over 20% to around 15% today. However, these figures are distorted by a large number of people working illegally or moonlighting. Reducing unemployment is the most urgent task facing the government and one on which all politicians are agreed.

Unemployment *(el paro)* is particularly high among young people in Spain and is the highest in the EU. Around 45% of those aged 16 to 19 (of those not still in education) and over 30% of those aged 20 to 24 are out of work. Even about 20% of university graduates are unemployed.

Unemployment is extremely expensive for the country as Spain has a relatively high social security benefit. One positive factor from the high level of unemployment has been that it has reversed the trend of people wanting to leave the countryside and move to the cities. Many people are staying in their villages to try to earn a living from the land.

In 1950, half of the work force was employed in agriculture, forestry or fishing. Today, two-thirds are employed in providing services and one-third are employed in industry. Only a small number are employed in agriculture.

Read the information on pages 68 and 69 and complete the quiz.

1 At what age can people start working in Spain? Is this a good or bad idea?
2 Where do most young people work, if they work?
3 In what ways is the normal working day changing?
4 How many days paid holiday do Spanish people get on average? How does this compare with the UK?
5 What happens during August to some businesses?
6 What are *'pagas extraordinarias'*? Do we have something similar in UK?
7 What is *'el paro'*?
8 What does Spain have the most of in Europe?
9 What positive fact is given about unemployment?

Trade unions

Spain used to be a country that had more strikes *(huelgas)* and lost more working days than any other country in the EU. However, unions have lost a lot of their bargaining power, partly owing to the high unemployment rate. Despite the squeezes on pay rises, enforced so that Spain could qualify for the single currency, there has been little industrial unrest in the last few years.

Spain has a fairly self-sufficient labour market and a skilled workforce who enjoy an affluent lifestyle compared with a few decades ago. Working conditions are generally good. There are pockets of unskilled foreign workers allowed in to the country to work in agriculture; they are mainly from North Africa.

Women at work

Under Franco, women were not allowed to work or even get a passport without permission from their father or husband, and not many women studied at university. This was quickly put right in the new constitution of 1978. Later, in 1987 and 1993, the First and Second Plans for Equal Opportunities for Women gave women a professional and salary equality with men, although they still mostly work in low-paid jobs. They earn about 26% less than the average male.

The number of working women in Spain has increased considerably in the last twenty years or so, with some 40% of women under 40 now in full-time or part-time work. Spain celebrates *el Día de la Mujer* (Day for the working woman) on 8 March and there are associations for female employees in most provinces.

Jobs for life

Many people try to complete very hard exams *(oposiciones)* in order to get into State employment, as this tends to give them a job for life. The exams can be taken twice a year for jobs ranging from postal workers to university professors. People pay private tutors *(preparadores)* or take courses via the Internet or distance learning, paying up to 700€ for a course. However, only about 40% are prepared sufficiently and many are disappointed as there are only about 14 000 placements available each year.

Many people still continue in their old habits of holding down more than one job *(pluriempleo)* and working overtime and extra shifts in order to pay their bills.

From 2004, 25 countries belong to the Europe Union. The citizens of these countries have a basic right to work freely in any country within this community.

INEM

Spain has a State-run National Employment Institute *(Instituto Nacional de Empleo* or *INEM)*. It operates about 700 offices *(oficinas de empleo)*, listing both national and local jobs and offering a comprehensive career resource library. Often, they will appoint personal counsellors to help people find work.

An interesting way of working

The *Mondragón Corporación Cooperativa (MCC)* began in the town of Mondragón in 1956. A group of young engineers were encouraged by their socialist priest, Father Jose María Arizmediarreta, to set up a co-operative to make paraffin cooking stoves. Today, it is one of the twelve largest employers in Spain, with over 160 employee-owned co-operatives involving 23 000 members.

Their philosophy is to establish a new business with a group of friends because they think that friendship forms the basis of good working relationships. The workers have their own bank, a research institute, insurance, social security, schools and colleges, and their own health system. Statistics show the Mondragón experiment to be twice as profitable as average businesses, with productivity surpassing any other organisation.

▼ The Spanish Stock Exchange

In January 1986, Spain became a member of the European Union, from which it has benefited greatly. Today, Spain is one of its most committed members. It has the fifth largest economy in Europe and accounts for 10% of EU output. Spain's most important industries include tourism, chemicals and petro-chemicals, heavy industry, such as iron and steel castings, food and beverages, and electrical and automobile manufacturing. The main growth areas are tourism, insurance, property development, electronics and financial services.

Read the information on pages 70 and 71 and complete the quiz.

1 What is the Spanish word for 'strike'?
2 Do you think it is important for workers to be allowed to go on strike?
3 Who are the unskilled workers in Spain?
4 How has working life changed for women in Spain?
5 What is the *INEM* and how does it work?
6 Use the Internet or library to find out more about the Mondragón Corporation. Where is Mondragón? Is there anything similar in the UK? Do you think it is a good idea?

18 Industry and commerce

Tourism

Perhaps more than any other industry, tourism has had the greatest influence on changing Spain from a poor and inward-looking society to the vibrant forward-looking country it is today. In 1959, there were under 3 million tourists visiting each year, but by 1973 the number had soared to over 34 million. Today, there are over 50 million tourists a year.

Since the Second World War, tourism has grown due to greater prosperity in northern European countries, along with increased leisure time and the taste for foreign travel. This is also coupled with cheaper air travel, which is cheaper today than ever before. Today, tourism earns around 10% of Spain's Gross Domestic Product (GDP) and employs over 10% of the total workforce. About 60% of Spain's GDP is in the service sector, of which most is related to tourism.

Most of the visitors are from the EU, including 14 million from the UK. The most popular resorts are along the *costas*, and the Balearic and Canary Islands.

Recently, Spain has tried to improve its image by promoting its vast cultural heritage and green eco-tourism in order to move away from the stereotypical image of people coming to Spain simply to enjoy the sun. This has had the added benefit of spreading the income generated from tourism more evenly throughout the country.

Tourism has also helped to keep many traditional arts and crafts alive for which Spain has been famous for centuries. Toledo has always been renowned for its steel swords and cutlery with intricate inlaid gold called *damasquinado*. Today, the jewellery is equally popular. Leather from Cordoba was likewise much sought after in Europe and still is today. Spanish lace work has always been renowned worldwide.

Agriculture

Although dependency on agriculture has diminished, Spain is still the world's greatest producer of olive oil. Spain has a 2000-year-old history of wine producing and has over 8 million hectares of vineyards – more than any country in the world, even France, although it is only the fourth largest producer of wine grapes and ranks third in wine production.

Spain ranks fifth in the world in book production. However, half of all Spanish people don't read books!

Spain ranks third in the world for fruit production and first in Europe for citrus fruits. Spain has an advantage over the rest of Europe because of a very early start to the growing season, therefore it can get ahead in the market.

Fashion

The fashion industry in Spain has grown in recent years. Madrid's fashion week – *la pasarela de Cibeles* – promotes world fashion as well as home-grown designers.

Cristóbal Balenciaga (1895–1972) was the first of many famous names to go to Paris and create a reputation for revolutionary and spectacular designs.

Paco Rabanne (Rabaneda) was born in San Sebastián. He first studied architecture in Paris before becoming a leader of high fashion with a particular eye for space-age styles and strange materials.

Adolfo Domínguez started life as a film-maker and author before turning his hand to designing clothes.

Spanish leather goods are excellent quality – the best known being **Loewe**.

Names to watch out for:

Vittorio y Luchino
Agatha Ruiz de la Prada
Mango
Zara

Read the information on pages 72 and 73 and complete the quiz.

1 How many British tourists visit Spain each year?
2 Is tourism a good thing or a bad thing. Discuss.
3 What has Spain done to improve its tourist image recently?
4 Traditional crafts are still important today. Use the Internet or library to find out about Lladró porcelain, lace making and embroidery, guitars and inlaid woodwork.
5 Give three facts about Spain's wine production.
6 What advantage do Spanish fruit growers have over the rest of Europe?
7 Find out some more about the fashion designers listed above.

Spain has never been a highly industrialised nation, except perhaps in Catalonia and the North. In Asturias and the Basque country, iron ore and coal made the steel industry an important one. Spain still produces much of its own steel, although, in general terms, it is moving towards more high-tech industries. Barcelona is regarded as Spain's economic powerhouse.

During the period between 1961 and 1973, known as *'los años de desarrollo'* ('years of development'), Spain's economy grew at 7%, faster than any country in the non-communist world except for Japan. Spain ranked as the world's ninth industrial power.

In the last thirty years, Spain has been transformed from a rural agricultural-based economy into a land with a diversified economy and strong manufacturing and service sectors.

The **motor industry** is one of Spain's major manufacturing industries. Although a lot of cars sold in Spain today are imported, many are manufactured in Spain but carry foreign names, such as Renault and Ford, as these large companies have set up factories there. SEAT is the nearest Spain ever got to having its own market. The Spanish government originally set it up in joint ownership with the Italian company, Fiat, but it is now fully owned by Volkswagen. Pegaso used to make elegant powerful cars, as did Hispano Suiza, but today it is mainly known for its lorries.

Spain has had a motorcycle industry for a long time, with names such as Derbi, Bultaco and Montesa being the best known. Caetano build coaches and the Basque firm Irízar Buses exports to over 44 countries and has factories in countries as far away as China, Mexico and Brazil. CASA aerospace company is part of the European Airbus industry along with France, Germany and the UK.

Did you know that...

- The car brand Mercedes was named after the Spanish wife and daughter of Herr Benz.
- The first submarine was designed and built by Isaac Peral between 1884 and 1887.
- Basque engineer Alejandro Goicoechea invented the *TALGO (Tren Articulado Ligero Goicoechea y Oriol)* in the early 1920s.
- The *autogiro* (the forerunner of the helicopter) was invented in the early 1920s by a Spanish aeronautical engineer called Juan de la Cierva.

Fishing

Spain has traditionally had a thriving fishing industry. It has the second largest fishing fleet in the world after Japan. However, when Spain joined the EU, it had to halve its fishing fleet to meet requirements, causing great trauma and hardship to whole communities. Spaniards spend almost as much on fish as they do on meat, consuming about 30kg of fish or seafood a year per person, twice as much as the average European. The fishing industry alone employs over 100 000 people, not including those employed in the canning and processing businesses.

Shipbuilding

Spain was one of the world's leading shipbuilding nations, rivalling Japan and South Korea, particularly in super tankers, aircraft carriers and amphibious support ships. The Bazán company still has a worldwide reputation in computer design and construction methods.

Wind turbines near Tarifa

Power

Franco had over 1 000 dams built in order to power Spain's industrial regeneration with cheap electricity. However, Spain is still too dependent on imported oil, which comes mainly from the former colony of Spanish Sahara.

Increasingly, natural gas is being exploited and coal is still quite important. There is a newer focus on renewable energy sources, such as wind and solar power. Campsa, the national petroleum company, and Repsol are both involved with the multinational chemical sector.

High-tech industries

The government has set up a number of schemes to encourage and promote high-tech industries. The Industrial Technological Development Centre *(Centro de Desarrollo Tecnológico Industrial* or *CDTI)* helps companies in international programmes, such as in the European Space Agency (ESA) where Spain's first astronaut, Pedro Duque, trained and worked.

Read the information on pages 74 and 75 and complete the quiz.

1 Can Spain be described as a highly industrialised nation? Explain your answer.
2 What years were important in the development of Spanish trade?
3 What are the more industrialised regions of Spain? What do they produce?
4 Use a dictionary to write a list of Spain's most important industries.
5 Is the motor industry important in Spain? Explain your answer.
6 What changes are taking place in the power industry?
7 Discuss how important you think it is for countries to develop renewable energy sources.

ATLANTIC OCEAN
(Océano Atlántico)
Bay of Biscay
(Golfo de Vizcaya)
FRANCE
(Francia)
PYRENEES
ANDORRA
PORTUGAL
SPAIN
(España)
CORDILLERA CANTABRICA
SIERRA CABRERA
SIERRA DE GUADARRAMA
SIERRA DE GREDOS
MONTES DE TOLEDO
SIERRA MORENA
SIERRA DE SEGURA
SIERRA NEVADA
SIERRA DE RONDA
El Ferrol
La Coruña
Carballo
Villalba
Santiago de Compostela
Lugo
Fonsagrada
Tineo
Oviedo
Gijón
Llanes
Santander
Reinosa
Bilbao
San Sebastián
Mondragón
Vitoria
Pamplona
Villablino
La Vecilla
Sarria
Lalin
Sil
Monforte de Lemos
León
Astorga
Miño
Orense
Vigo
La Gudina
Baltar
Esla
Villada
Palencia
Valderas
Osorno
Burgos
Logroño
Ebro
Arga
Gállego
Cinca
Pico de Aneto
Llobregat
Figueras
Gerona
Manresa
Tarrasa
Barcelona
Costa Brava
Soria
Valladolid
Duero
Saragossa
Lérida
Zamora
Medina del Campo
Tormes
Salamanca
Segovia
Jalón
Caspe
Reus
Tarragona
Costa Dorada
Tortosa
Tajuna
Avila
Guadalajara
Tajo
Morella
Vinaroz
Cuidad Rodrigo
Béjar
Alcalá de Henares
MADRID
Teruel
Mijares
Hoyos
Jarandilla
Plasencia
Cuenca
Castellón
Turia
Toledo
Lliria
Sagunto
Costa del Azahar
Cáceres
Trujillo
Requena
Valencia
Júcar
Guadiana
Daimiel
Villarrobledo
Ciudad Real
Manzanares
Albacete
Alcira
Badajoz
Don Benito
Valdepeñas
Almansa
Alcoy
Almendralejo
Puertollano
Alcaraz
Segura
Yecla
Jumilla
Alicante
Pozoblanco
Azuaga
La Carolina
Linares
Moratalla
Cieza
Elche
Orihuela
Cehegín
Murcia
Constantina
Córdoba
Guadalquivir
Jaén
Martos
Totana
Nerva
Lorca
Cartagena
Alcala la Real
Baza
Águilas
Puente
Seville
Marchen
Genil
Guadix
Huércal Overa
Huelva
Osuna
Granada
Costa Blanca
Costa de la Luz
Cerro de Mulhacén
Morón de la Frontera
Antequera
Almería
Jerez de la Frontera
Arcos
Ronda
Malaga
Motril
Berja
Cádiz
Marbella
Costa del Sol
Gibraltar
Algeciras
Strait of Gibraltar
(Estrecho de Gibraltar)
Cueta
Melilla
MEDITERRANEAN SEA
(Mar Mediterráneo)
Menorca
Mahón
Mallorca
Palma
Manacor
Ibiza
Ibiza Town
Formentera
BALEARIC ISLANDS
(Islas Baleares)
ALGERIA
(Argelia)
MOROCCO
(Marruecos)
ATLANTIC OCEAN
CANARY ISLANDS
(Islas Canarias)
GRACIOSA
LANZAROTE
LA PALMA
Santa Cruz de Tenerife
FUERTEVENTURA
Las Palmas de Gran Canaria
GOMERA
TENERIFE
HIERRO
GRAN CANARIA
0 50 100 150 200 Miles
0 50 100 150 200 250 300 Kilometres

USA
(Estados Unidos
de Norteamérica)
México
Cuba
República
Dominicana
Puerto Rico
Guatemala
Honduras
El Salvador
Nicaragua
Costa Rica
Panamá
Venezuela
Colombia
Ecuador
Peru
Bolivia
Paraguay
Chile
Uruguay
Argentina
Spain
(España)
Ceuta
Melilla
Guinea
Ecuatorial
Filipinas

Useful Spanish websites

Central Tourist Office
www.tourspain.es

Autonomous Communities
Each one has its own website:
Andalucía - www.andalucia.org
Aragón - www.staragon.com
Asturias - www.infoasturias.com
Baleares - www.caib.es
Canarias - www.saturno-canarias.org
Cantabria - www.turismo.cantabria.org
Castilla-La Mancha - www.jccm.es
Castilla-León - www.jcyl.es
Catalunya - www.gencat.es
Ceuta - www.ciceuta.es
Comunidad Valenciana - www.comunidad-valenciana.org
Extremadura - www.juntaex.es
Galicia - www.turgalicia.es
Madrid - www.comadrid.es
Melilla - www.melilla.com
Murcia - www.murcia-turismo.com
Navarra - www.navarra.es
País Vasco - www.euskadi.net
La Rioja - www.larioja.org

Instituto Andaluz de la Juventud - IAJ
Useful general information for young people
www.juntadeandalucia.es
www.andaluciajunta.es/patiojoven

ClubPop
General information for 18–28 year olds
www.club-pop.es

Employment Office
www.inem.es

Magazines
www.bravoporti.com

Environmental issues
www.mma.es *(Ministerio de Medio Ambiente) Ministry for Environment*
www.gyj.es - *Geo magazine, like* National Geographic

Job search website
www.infojobs.net

Spanish national railways
www.renfe.es

National newspaper - El País
www.elpais.es

General interest magazines
www.muyinteresante.es
www.quo.wanadoo.es
www.cambio16.info

Statistics office
www.ine.es

General information
www.red2000.com/spain
www.SiSpain.org
www.spainview.com

Television weekly
www.semana.es

Index

air travel 53
agriculture 73
Andalusia 34
apartment blocks 12
art 49, 66
Almodóvar 67
athletics 23
autonomous regions/communities 61–62

Balearic Islands 35
Barcelona 47
bars 25
Basque people and country 36
Bilbao 46
birth rate 11
birthdays 8
breakfast 9, 24
bullfighting 30
buses 55

cafés 25
Canary Islands 35
Catalan 7, 37
Catholicism 10
Ceuta 35
cheese 27
Christmas 29
cinema 67
cities 46–47, 48–51
Civil War 58
climate 32
coffee 26
Comunidad Autónoma 61-62
Consejo municipal 63
costumes 28
countryside 33, 40
currency 6
customs 28-29
cycling 23

daily routine 9
Dalí 66
death penalty 62
diet 24
dinner 24
dishes 27
divorce 10
drinks 26
driving 52

El Greco 66
elderly 10
elections 62, 63
emigration 38
environment 41
ethnic groups 36–39
examinations 18, 19
Expo '92 7

family book 10
family life 8–11
farming 42, 73
fast food 25
fashion 73
ferry 53
festivals 28
first communion 8
fishing industry 75
flags 6, 61
flamenco 30
folk music, dances 30, 31
food 24, 25
football 20
Franco 58

Galician 36
Gaudí 47
gazpacho 27
geographical features 32, 33
Gibraltar 34
Golden Age 56
golf 22
government 60
Goya 66
gypsies 39

health 11
history 56–59
holiday homes 15
holidays 21, 68
homes 12–13
houses 14, 15
hydro-electric power 75

immigration 38
industry 72–75
islands 35

jobs 68–69
Juan Carlos I 6, 60

kings 57

landscapes 42
languages 7
leaders 57
leisure activities 20–23
lottery 31
lunch 24

Madrid 48–51
magazines 65
markets 44
marriage 8
mayor 63
meals 24
media 64
Melilla 35

metro 50, 55
Miró 66
Mondragón 71
monuments 6
Moors 56
motor sport 22
motorways 52
music 20

names 9
national holiday 7
newspapers 65
nicknames 9

old quarter 44
oranges 26

paella 27
paradores 21
parks 45, 49
parliament 63
patio 13
pelota 23
people 36–37
pets 8
Picasso 66
political parties 59, 60
politics 59
pollution 41
population 42
power 75
Prime Minister 63
provinces 62

Queen Isabel 57

radio 64
railways 50, 54
regional autonomies 61
religion 10
restaurants 25
rivers 4, 32
roads 52
Romans 56
Royal Family 60

Sepharad 7, 59
Seville 46
school holidays 16
school leaving certificate 18
school subjects 16, 17, 18
school system 16-18
sea travel 53
shipbuilding 75
shops 45
Sierra Nevada 32
social housing 15
sport 20, 21, 22–23
squatters 15
suburbs 46
superstitions 31
supper 24

tapas 25
technology 75
television 64
tennis 22
theme parks 21
toll roads 52
tourism 39, 72
towns 44–47
trade unions 70
traditions 28, 29
trains 54
trams 55
transport 52-55
taxis 55

unemployment 69
university 19

Valencia 46
vegetarianism 26
Velazquez 66
villages 43

water sports 23
weather 32
wine 26, 73
women 70
working life 68, 69
world language 5